Order My Steps

492 days

My GBS Story

Order My Steps

492 days

My GBS Story

Todd McGuire

Order My Steps: 492 Days, My GBS Story

Todd McGuire

Copyright Pending 2022

All rights reserved. This publication may not be reproduced, stored in an electronic system, or transmitted in any form or by any means, electronic, mechanical, photocopy, recording, or otherwise, without proper credit to the author. Brief quotations may be used without permission.

Most Scripture quotations are from The King James Version of the Bible unless otherwise specified.

Amplified Bible (AMP) Copyright © 2015 by The Lockman Foundation, La Habra, CA 90631.

Woodsong Publishing
5989 Spring Meadow Lane
Seymour, IN 47274

www.woodsongpublishing.com
woodsongpublishing@yahoo.com

Printed in the United States of America

ISBN 979-8-9855200-6-4

Table Of Contents

Foreword
Chapter 1: TRUST
Chapter 2: LAUNCH OUT
Chapter 3: LIVING BY FAITH
Chapter 4: THE VALLEY OF SHADOWS
Chapter 5: "I HAVE ORDERED YOUR STEPS"
Chapter 6: THE STORM HAS BEGUN
Chapter 7: WE ARE NOT ALONE
Chapter 8: TREATMENT BEGINS
Chapter 9: FEAR IS A LIAR
Chapter 10: YOU'VE GOT TO GO DOWN BEFORE YOU CAN GO UP
Chapter 11: HALLUCINATIONS
Chapter 12: YOU'RE IN TROUBLE MISTER!
Chapter 13: I'M A HUMAN PINCUSHION
Chapter 14: NEW BEGINNINGS
Chapter 15: I'VE REFIRED
Chapter 16: I WANT TO GO HOME
Chapter 17: FLY DAY
Chapter 18: I'M SO GLAD TO BE IN CANADA
Chapter 19: LONGING FOR NORMALCY
Chapter 20: SETBACK
Chapter 21: MY SMILE IS GONE
Chapter 22: HEAVENLY IVIG
Chapter 23: MOVING DAY
Chapter 24: I'M FINALLY HERE
Chapter 25: CHECK YOUR PRIVACY AT THE DOOR
Chapter 26: GETTING INTO A NEW ROUTINE
Chapter 27: ANNIVERSARY CELEBRATIONS INSTITUTION STYLE
Chapter 28: WHAT AM I DOING IN A WHEELCHAIR?
Chapter 29: FINDING THE SILVER LINING IN EVERY CLOUD
Chapter 30: WE ARE PROGRESSING
Chapter 31: CABBIE YOGA
Chapter 32: CELEBRATE EVERY SMALL VICTORY
Chapter 33: A HUGE STEP TO FREEDOM
Chapter 34: NEVER GIVE UP
Chapter 35: PRAYING FRIENDS ARE INVALUABLE
Chapter 36: LIVING ON THE EDGE
Chapter 37: HEALTHIER THAN I'VE EVER BEEN

Foreword

A beautiful inspirational story recounting Rev. T. D. McGuire's 492-day journey and miraculous recovery from Guillain-Barre syndrome.

This author, who has had a proven and fruitful ministry for over twenty-five years, went through a grueling struggle, that took him to death's door, but in this process he has helped countless others experience a more abundant life. When God saw this man's faith, He showed up and did amazing things.

His writing makes you reflect on what's really important and reminds us of the many things that we often take for granted until we lose them.

I'm truly honored to call T.D. McGuire and his extremely supportive wife my friends. I'm certain that his story will encourage many people. If you're like me, you will weep at times and, also, enjoy a good laugh while your heart is filled to overflowing with thanksgiving and praise to our almighty God. Oh, the surpassing greatness of God's faithfulness and favor!

When your steps are ordered of the Lord, you can't help but pay attention as His blessings chase you down and overtake you. Every setback becomes a setup for a comeback. God's touch of favor changes everything! It's not by our own strength or by our own power. It's because Almighty God, the One who holds our future in His hands, goes before us, fighting our battles, making crooked places straight, blessing us indeed, and enlarging our territory so that His Kingdom can be expanded.

I encourage you to trust God as this author has done. You, too, can have the strength and determination to overcome every obstacle, outlast every challenge, and come through every difficulty better off than you were before. Our God has a master plan that He has designed for our lives. There are times when we don't understand where He's taking us, but we must trust Him, knowing that He is working it all out for our advantage and His Glory!

Rev. Jonathan Cole – Amherst, Nova Scotia

Chapter 1
Trust

Do you trust me?

> Trust in the Lord with all thine heart; and lean not unto thine own understanding. In all thy ways acknowledge him, and He shall direct thy paths.
>
> Proverbs 3:5-6

Trusting God is a concept many Christians know about, and we attempt to live out. Some have no choice but to trust God as they live in dire, extreme circumstances.

We observed this firsthand as we went on a missions trip to Nigeria, Africa in the fall of 2003. We saw people with nothing much, as far as this world's goods are concerned, but who had an amazing trust in God and lifted up a hearty praise to God!

We attended a conference in the jungle, where locals and nationals had walked to get there. They worshiped God from morning to night, sleeping on the benches and floor. We observed a fevered baby being held out to us to be prayed for. The baby's fever broke as God touched the little one. We saw some who couldn't reach us, touch our shoe with one hand, and with the other hand they touched their own foreheads as they prayed in faith believing. I'd never seen such faith!!

It's amazing to me that in the most poverty-stricken countries, that's where we see the greatest hunger for God. Really, though, it's no mystery, as we North Americans tend to lean upon our "stuff" too much and lean less on God.

Our family has always leaned upon the Lord, or so we thought, but God had a college course of trust for us to study in.

Penny and I met at Northeast Christian College in 1995. We both had felt the Lord leading us to ministry and applied for the same Bible college. We fell in love that winter, we got engaged and were married the following April. We then began to attempt to follow the leading of God. God then blessed us with two children; Desirèe born in 1997 and Christopher, born in 1998, We Pastored for seventeen years while raising our little family. After twenty-two years together, we thought we knew what trust was. Little did we know that we were about to face some troubling times in the next couple of years, even before I eventual battled with GBS.

In August of 2015, I had a neat experience happen to me. Penny and I had been in that particular pastorate for nine years, and one Sunday afternoon, while I was locking the church door, I felt God speak to me and ask me a direct question.

He said; "Do you trust me?" I immediately responded, "Yes Lord, I trust you!" I waited and there was no response.

The following Wednesday evening, after midweek service,

ORDER MY STEPS

I was locking the church door again, and I felt God speak to me again, and ask; "Do you trust me?" I immediately again responded, "Yes Lord, I trust you! I waited and there was no response.

The very next Sunday afternoon, while I was locking the church door, again, I felt God speak to me and ask me the same question, but with emphasis on my name; "Todd, Do you trust me?" I immediately responded; "Yes, Lord, I trust you!" Then I asked, "What is this all about?" I waited and there was no response.

Right around the same time, a lay minister in our church, John McMullin, had come up to Penny, one evening during prayer at the church, and said to her, "Sis, God is wanting you to trust Him more." It seems God was giving us both the same message, loud and clear!

We had settled into our Pastoral role and things were going good. Penny and I were also working full-time jobs to supplement our income as we now had a daughter in college. We were also out more doing concerts and that branch of our ministry was growing.

On July 24th, 2016, we had a children's evangelist come by, and they had done a tremendous job, but something was unsettled in my spirit. I was at the front, praying with some of the children, when I went quietly by myself to a corner to pray. I asked God to show me what this is about. Was there someone needing prayer? Was I supposed to give a word to someone? The Lord quietly spoke and said, "It is time." I did not have to ask Him what He meant. As soon as He said it, I knew. Our time there as pastor had come to a close.

I spoke with Penny about it, and she felt the same thing.

She had placed her total trust in me and any decision about leaving.

God has something for us, but what? I spoke that evening and gave my resignation, effective the beginning of September, exactly ten years to the day that we started Pastoring that location.

We began the moving process from the life that we had built, to our house we had purchased a few years prior in Perth-Andover, NB. We were excited and nervous at the same time as we were to start a full-time Evangelistic ministry. This was something that we always dreamed would take place, however, we never knew the time that it would begin. The doors before us were beginning to open. We were enjoying the freedom to minister in different places, and things were taking off for the McGuires.

Chapter 2
Launch Out

In January of 2017, we left for our music tour. We had only three confirmed dates. We truly were blazing a trail into new and uncharted territory. We picked up a few more bookings, while on the road. We had a great time, connecting and getting to know new people, and building relationships. We visited three different RV Parks, and the folks seemed to enjoy our music. We only had a short window of opportunity, as we just a had a few weeks abroad, and then we had to be back on our home soil to continue our tour.

I began to pray while we were on the road home. "Lord, you need to do something big for us to help expand our ministry borders!"

I also began praying the prayer of Jabez.

> And Jabez called on the God of Israel, saying, Oh that thou wouldest bless me indeed, and enlarge my coast, and that thine hand might be with me, and that thou wouldest keep me from evil, that it may not grieve me! And God granted him that which he requested.
> 1 Chronicles 4:10 KJV

During the spring and summer of 2017, our calendar was full. We made a lot of awesome connections! God was moving us ahead and doing the miraculous on our home soil. Our bills were being paid but not a lot to spare. We were putting an extreme amount of miles on our vehicle, and the offerings were lower than what we needed to keep things moving like we had to. I knew that God would supply, and we needed Him to intervene on our behalf. We made it through the Christmas season, and I made a New Year's resolution for 2018.

I resolved to do the will of God, if it killed me.

Together, we had been praying this prayer for these three things since 2016:
- Health
- That souls would be added to the Kingdom
- Provision and favor

Chapter 3
Living By Faith

We were just a few days from departing again for another tour abroad, and there was nothing secure as far as a place to stay. We did not own a motor home or a travel trailer. We knew God would have it worked out; I just had to prove to Him that I trusted Him.

I had been praying that the Lord would work something out for us. Tuesday evening, we received a call from a very kind gentleman, Dana Delong, who believed in us. He allowed us to stay in his trailer, in a 55 plus park, where our uncle also stays, for one month.

We left on Thursday, January eighteenth, for an annual conference in Louisiana, called Because Of The Times. There was a promise of over 2500 ministers there from around the world, and we desperately needed to make connections and get bookings. We had one stop in Mississippi. Although they had another evangelist booked, the Pastor said that they would put us up in a hotel and take care of some meals. We were sincerely grateful for the hospitality of that church and were booked to come back to them in the month of March.

Most people do not see the other side of ministry: the worry, the stress, the financial burden that it takes just to get down the road, and then trying to juggle finances to keep everything back home afloat. I'm not complaining at all, as God has blessed us, but let me just share something with you. We literally had eight hundred American dollars for gas, meals, and hotels for 3 people, as our son also travelled with us. Hopefully, we didn't have any mechanical issues! We drove two thousand plus miles on that money and still had one thousand miles to go, and we had very few bookings.

Is that called insane faith, or stupidity? Either way, we were fully trusting in God! We met up with Rev. Buck Treadway, a wonderful elder minister whom we look up to greatly, and he promoted us heavily, talking us up to everyone that he knew. He introduced us to many people and for that we thank him!

We arrived in Florida, January thirtieth, and settled into our 1979, Holiday Rambler trailer. Bookings began to slowly trickle in. My stress level and anxiety were High! In the last few days, I had our Blue Cross health care plan payment bounce, our cellphone bill back in Canada was overdue, and our travel insurance needed to be topped up. Where was I going to get the finances for that? I had two traveling with me. It would be easier for one, but we were a group and family.

February came, and things were picking up nicely, and we had made several wonderful connections; however, I had been sick with an upper respiratory illness for a couple weeks and it really did not want to let go. I'd been treating it with over-the-counter medication and trying to rest, but we were going nonstop from morning till night.

We had a booking at one of the local RV parks, and we came home from that almost broke and very discouraged. We were road weary and worn, and I was exhausted physically and mentally. Stress was taking its toll on me. When we got our gear unpacked, I called a quick family meeting, because

ORDER MY STEPS

honestly, I was ready to throw in the towel and go home! Chris, our son, spoke up through his tears and said; "Dad, I'm sleeping on the floor in a trailer...I believe in us!"

We prayed and stayed.... God met us in our need! We had picked up several more bookings, and we left on Thursday, March eighth for Mississippi. We would be staying at a church evangelist quarters, and we had bookings between there and Louisiana. We were excited to leave for Texas in April, which was an incredible open door and more uncharted territory. Beyond The Open Door

Chapter 4
The Valley Of Shadows

Diary entry: March 4th

Over the last few days I have been experiencing lower leg weakness and numbness in my hands and feet. My extremities feel heavy like I'm carrying cement blocks. I'm not sure what's wrong. I don't want to tell Penny as I don't want to worry her. I'm hoping it's a pinched nerve from lugging the heavy equipment around.

We had a service at Faith World, in Leesburg, FL. We arrived early and began to set up our gear, and I could not feel my feet, as they were numb. I continued to set up and greet people even though I was perplexed with what was happening. We finished with the service, and we had an incredible time in God, but now, both my legs were numb. However, they seemed to be ok when I would sit down, after a few minutes. We went out with the Pastor, and his family to eat, but something still wasn't right. We travelled back to the trailer, after our lunch, and had the evening to rest.

Monday morning, we had to go do some business near Orlando, which meant a couple hours drive for us, there and back. Later that evening, we decided, after a long weekend of traveling and concerts, that we should visit the ER at Zephyrhills Advent Hospital. By now, my calves had stopped working and my legs were terribly sore. It was an effort to make my legs work. I had to pull myself up a couple stairs. I thought this pain and uncomfortable feeling in my legs was from the exercise that I had been doing. Each night, and several times through the day, we would all go out on the bicycles and ride for health and exercise. Besides that, it was eighty degrees and beautiful!

An interesting addition here is that as Penny had driven by this same hospital different times, as it was on the main drag, God impressed her on three different occasions that "Before you leave Florida, you're going to be in that hospital!"

We made an ER visit for me as a precaution before heading off to Mississippi on Thursday. There were sick people around us everywhere, and I wondered why I was there? After all, I didn't "feel" sick. We registered and told the nurse my symptoms. The tests began. My blood pressure was good, my sugars were normal, my heart rate was on target. I seemed to be the picture of health, except for a little overweight detail.

The Doctor came in and assessed me. "How do you feel," he asked? "I feel great, other than that my hands and feet feel like cinder blocks," I replied. He ordered a Computerized Axial Tomography (CAT) scan, and he also wanted more blood work. His final diagnosis was that I possibly had diabetic neuropathy which causes your extremities to lose feeling. I was prescribed Gabapentin and sent home. I had been a diabetic for some years but was not on insulin, only a pill, which kept it under control.

Tuesday morning, I began to feel bad, like flu aches, except more intense. I spent the day in bed, as I had no energy, and I needed to rest as we were booked to leave in 2 days

ORDER MY STEPS

for Mississippi, Louisiana, and eventually, Texas. Penny and Chris were washing, cleaning, and packing in preparation for our departure to our next destination. I spend my time in prayer, asking God for a miracle. My thoughts included: I can't be sick; I do the bookings. I pay the bills. I get us where we need to be next. The responsibility of my family weighed heavily upon my shoulders.

Penny was leaving for the last trip to the laundromat to finish up the washing before we did our final packing. Chris was sitting quietly in the front room, and I couldn't help but think that he knew there was something seriously wrong: Dad's not doing good. He's been sick to his stomach several times today and can't feel his hands or feet. And now his walking is becoming increasingly difficult.

I took the Gabapentin, but it was too strong on my stomach and caused me to be sick, again.

I was taught from childhood, and in turn have taught others, to do what the Proverb says:

> Trust in the Lord with all your heart, And lean not on your own understanding; In all your ways acknowledge Him, And He shall direct your paths.
>
> Proverb 3:5

If you have a need, Jesus is the answer!
If you need a healing, Jesus is the answer!
If you have an issue, Jesus is the answer!

I was now leaning heavily on that verse and trusting in Him!

Chapter 5
"I Have Ordered Your Steps"

I called upon the name of the Lord in fervent intercession: "Lord, I need a miracle! Lord, I can't be sick. Touch my body!" That's when it happened! Whether or not you believe in Heaven, God, angelic beings, or anything of the like, let me tell you what I experienced.

I was transported spiritually to a room, and in this room, there were angels. They stood side by side and hovered about one foot off the ground. They were tall, at least eight feet, and they were dressed in white robes with a gold sash around their waists. In the center of this room was a 360-degree staircase, and at the top, there was a throne, and around that throne was the most pure and bright light you have ever seen, or could even imagine. I knew that it was God! What else could it be? I wondered, Am I in Heaven? I was suddenly filled with the most peaceful feeling that I had ever felt before!

As I prayed, hot tears flowed down my face: "Lord, I need a miracle! Lord, I can't be sick. Lord, please heal my body! I need a miracle, I need a miracle." I continued to repeat this prayer.

The angelic beings played brass instruments that looked to me like a mixture between a trombone and a trumpet: maybe like a long medieval bugle. On each instrument, there hung a small white banner, with green printing, and it was trimmed in gold. The sound that came out of the instruments, however, was symphonic! Not at all what you would expect, and it was a continuous, sustained, beautiful sound. I thought this strange, as humans must continuously take breaths in between notes. Angelic beings are supernatural and do not need to take such breaths.

I looked around the room and saw pillars, but the room was so large that I could not see a ceiling. The room was adorned in the most beautiful color of gold that I have ever seen. The best way that I have found to describe the color would be like the color of ginger ale. Everything was this color, including the stairs. I climbed to the third step up from the bottom, and I was overwhelmed by a feeling that, if I don't go back, I'm ok with that. It was the oddest feeling. I didn't want to leave Penny, our children, my folks, or any of our family for that matter, but it suddenly felt ok if I did.

That feeling of peace and comfort reminded me of a child in the arms of their grandmother who is gently rocking them in a rocking chair next to the wood stove, as she hums a lullaby. It was the feeling of security that everything is alright! Your worries are behind you, and you are totally safe.

As I sat trying to process all of this, God's robe came down toward me from the top of that stair case. It was a brown plush robe with gold inlays. I grabbed it, much like the woman with the issue of blood in the Bible did, out of complete desperation! Though I was still praying, I cried out to him!

I was gripping the hem of his garment in a death grip; "Lord, I need a miracle! Lord, I can't be sick! Touch my body! I need a healing!"

ORDER MY STEPS

At that very moment, He came down to me. I could not see an actual person, just the bright light as it surrounded me. I stood still, holding onto His garment, as God spoke to me.

"Todd, I have ordered your steps," were the words I heard.

"I have ordered your steps?" I rehearsed this in my head.

"I have ordered your steps?" This feeling of sheer delight overwhelmed me as I believed that I had been healed! The realization struck me that Isaiah the prophet of old was in this very spot, according to Scripture.

> In the year that king Uzziah died I saw also the Lord sitting upon a throne, high and lifted up, and his train filled the temple.
> Isaiah 6:1

I saw the train of God! I saw the throne of God! I was standing in Heaven's throne room with the angels and God!! He was speaking my name! He said He had ordered my steps! I thought, I must be healed!! Thank-you Jesus! I'm healed, I'm healed!!

I felt the hands of God touch my shoulders and turn me around. I faced a door in front of me, and I felt a garment being draped over my shoulders. I felt his hands fastening under my chin, on my chest. He spoke once more: "Now Go," and He gently pushed me towards the shimmering doorway.

Suddenly, I found myself sitting on the floor, in the tiny trailer doorway, in a fetal position. Our son came in and asked me, "Dad, are you ok?" He said, "You were praying with such fervency, and then it all went quiet. Dad, I thought you died!" I replied, "Son, I did not die, but I've been to heaven, and I can't wait to go back!"

Chapter 6
The Storm Has Begun

Diary entry: March 7, 2018

"Please storm heaven for us. Todd is being admitted to the hospital and undergoing multiple tests for muscle weakness to where he can't even walk. We need all who know how to pray, to do so. Thanks so much."

I got up that morning, unable to feel my right side from my foot to my shoulder. I drug my leg down the hallway to the restroom. I had to sit down, or I was going to fall. Once seated, I knew that I was not getting back up on my own. I tried a couple times, unsuccessfully. I had to call my family to rescue me. Once I was up, it took Penny around a half hour to help me get cleaned up and dressed. With their assistance, I leaned on a piece of musical equipment with wheels, Penny hung on to the waist of my pants, and I slowly wheeled to the door where our van was awaiting. I got into the vehicle and knew that if something didn't happen, I was not walking into the hospital. We arrived at the ER and Chris and Penny got me into a wheelchair. This was the last day of me walking and the first day of an eight-month hospital/rehabilitation stay.

This second visit and admission to the Hospital brought confusion to the staff as everything was normal except for the acute weakness in my lower extremities. More bloodwork and an MRI were ordered. I was admitted to the hospital as they knew I couldn't walk. It took a team of 3-4 men to get me onto the hospital bed, and in the process, I slipped down, almost onto the floor. After an interminable wait, I was wheeled up to my room.

The 5 am bloodwork began, as well as frequent checks, by the nursing staff. I can't say enough about how good the journey was when it came to the staff and the care we received. We only had one major incident that actually happened that Thursday morning.

Diary entry: March 8, 2018

"He goes into surgery. tomorrow morning. so a chest catheter can be put in. He will then undergo plasma therapy. Please continue to hold us all up in prayer He still has numbness in his hands. legs and mouth. He is mostly immobile. God will see us through We are so. so grateful for the Pastor that just showed up to visit with us pray for us. We Pastored for 18 years and are used to being on the other side of the bed but you sure appreciate a Man Of God showing up in your hour of need "

Thursday morning came to find wave after wave of emotions sweeping over us. What's wrong with me? Why can't I feel anything? It's getting worse. How long will it last? Will I ever walk again? All these questions flooded my mind. I tried to stay calm for my family's sake. This cannot be happening! My family's rock, provider, and leader had been struck down! What will we do, now?

The physiotherapy team showed up to assess my situation. Two little female physiotherapists that were no bigger than my legs came in. They introduced themselves and said, "Mr.

ORDER MY STEPS

McGuire, we want you to stand and see how far you can walk."

"Stand," I exclaimed!? "I can't stand, dear. I can't feel my legs or my feet!"

"We have brought this walker," she explained. "This will allow you to use your upper body strength to assist you."

I said, "Are you sure you want me to do this?" I knew very well what the outcome would be.

She said, "We will lift the bed and all you will have to do is scoot your bottom off the mattress and stand."

I did what I was told, as my wife has trained me well. I scooted off the bed, and it took all the strength that I could muster to stand. Immediately my arms began to shake.

The physiotherapist said, "Good! Now let's see if you can lift one leg and take a small step."

Step, I thought!! Step! I can't even feel where I'm walking, let alone step! But I did what I was told. The next thing I knew, I fell into the walker. The bars were now up under my arms and my toes were bent back in an awkward fashion. I could feel the pain in my feet as I screamed "I NEED TO LAY DOWN!"

"No, no, no!" The therapist exclaimed in a loud voice; "Don't lay down!" She was no doubt wondering how they would get me up. The walker gave way, and I threw myself, with as much ease as I could muster, onto the floor.
Upon my sudden impact with the floor, my intravenous was pulled out, and blood was going everywhere! The

physiotherapists were screaming! I was trying to get my bearings and rolled onto my back. Anyone who has spent time in a hospital knows that hospital gowns are not very modest, especially from the back. So, blood was coming out of my right arm, I was on the floor warming it with my bare backside, and they were calling, "MAN DOWN, MAN DOWN!" Code white was going out over the hospital p.a. ("code white" is a call for medical assistance, usually for a visitor or staff).

I began to see heads poke in the doorway, wondering what the fuss was all about. As they tried to come up with a plan on how to get me back up, I said; "Just give me a blanket. It's not that bad down here! I've already warmed up my spot!" After a few minutes, I saw two rugged men come in the door. "Finally," I said to myself, "someone my size to deal with someone my size!" Go figure! They managed to get a sheet under me, and with a lot of effort, they finally got me back into bed.

It didn't take the staff long at all to come in and put a pretty, yellow bracelet on my left arm, that read, "Fall Risk." Hello! I already told them that! The blessing out of all this was that my Neurologist, Dr. Aladdin Khan, was right there seconds after the fall happened. He approached me and immediately said, "We are canceling your lumbar puncture. Mr. McGuire, you have "Guillain-Barrè. I have seen this many times before."

I wasn't sure what Guillain-Barrè was, but I said; "If you need to put in another line to give me meds or some kind of a prescription, then go ahead! That way I can get out of here. Dr. Khan, said; "It's not that easy. GBS is a complicated sickness. It could last from 2 weeks, 2 months, or 2 years. It's very unpredictable!" Then he said the words that I didn't

ORDER MY STEPS

want to hear: "Whatever you have booked, cancel! You will be here till we figure some more things out."

And so, the journey began....

Chapter 7
We Are Not Alone

Unless you have been in another country, hospitalized far away from family and friends, then you have no idea the loneliness that can come with such a time. I was certainly glad to have my one and only Penelope with me. She is the love of my life and has stuck with me through the greatest trial that we have ever sustained. I was also glad to have our son, Christopher, there, as he was a strength for both Penny and me. We, however, did not have our daughter Desireè, or our parents and siblings. Anyone knows that when you are sick and potentially facing a life-threatening situation, family is the only thing that matters. It truly didn't matter to me if we ever booked another concert, or sang on the greatest of stages, as that's what we had been striving for. No, it didn't matter if we traveled another mile to get to the next venue or if we ever recorded another CD. Family was all I wanted and needed!

There were so many questions in my mind that I kept secret between God and myself (as if He didn't know), like: How long will I be laid up? How will I pay the bills from a hospital bed? Will we even have a house to come home to? Will I even make it home? Will we lose our vehicle? Will I have to go bankrupt? You see, I didn't have a backup plan. That is totally ludicrous to some of you reading this, but not to this writer. We didn't have a fat investment that we could cash in or a 401K to live off. We didn't have a savings account to glean from. No, God called us out to this ministry, and He was just going to have to take care of things until I was well again. That's called "blind faith," and let me tell you that it is not for the faint of heart, either! I never truly knew what God meant a few years earlier when he challenged me with the question, "Do you Trust Me?" You see, I never truly understood the word "trust" until this very moment: living completely on faith with no guaranteed weekly income.

If you think that the life of a southern gospel artist or evangelist is easy, try it! Leave your job, career, family, friendships, home, and country, and set out into the unknown with nothing but a minuscule amount of money. I'm talking just enough to get you to your next destination, maybe. And do that for weeks and months on end. Then come back to me and tell me that it's glorious!

You see that I was not born with a silver spoon in my mouth, nor do we have a family name that is nationally or internationally known. I mean, who is Todd McGuire? Who are the McGuires? I suddenly began to feel alone and broken. This is the first time that I have shared these thoughts publicly, but let me say this, I don't have a hard luck story to tell! God has been good to me and to the McGuires! Within 2 to 3 days, God began to move upon the hearts of friends, fellow colleagues, and acquaintances around the world. Funds began to come in by way of E-Transfer, a GoFundMe account, as well as a compassion fund, along with checks and cash. We also were privileged to receive letters of encouragement, visits from pastors and saints alike, and total strangers that I had never met before.

People that were vacationing in the sunny south began to stop by, and one by one, God showed up! Word began to spread. We were making news everywhere! People back home began to rally, churches took up offerings, fellow artists and friends, alike, planned benefit concerts. I was at a loss for words, and even in my deteriorating state, I knew that if I didn't survive, that people back home had Penny's back.

I could then, with that knowledge, allow this sickness to begin to run its course. No one really knew what the outcome was going to be: we just trusted God! Those six little words that God had spoken to me in His throne room kept us going! We knew we were going to come out of this trial, we just didn't know when.

Let me take the time, at the closing of this chapter, to thank you a million times over for being so kind to us. We are forever indebted to those who prayerfully and financially have supported us. We sincerely love and appreciate you all! When God removed me as the provider from the equation, and said, "let me show you what I can do without you." His people stepped up!

Chapter 8
Treatment Begins

Friday morning, after their daily meeting on what to do with me, the doctors came in to visit. They do this with every case that they're assigned. I knew that I was in good hands. I had 5 doctors, and specialists in their respective fields, working on me. Dr. Khan, my neurologist, announced that there were 2 options on combatting GBS. They could do a series of Immuno Globulin treatments (IVIG), which was something I did receive later, back in Canada, or they could hit it aggressively with a dialysis treatment called Plasma Pheresis. He chose the latter of the two, as they preferred to do this treatment first, as it's more aggressive. They booked the operating room for later that morning to insert a Dialysis Catheter into my heart. After they prepped me for surgery, Penny and I took a chance for a photo opportunity, and it was then that I decided, and announced, that we needed to make our whole journey public. We had lived a very public life in ministry, and so, it was just another way to reach out to others: to continue to encourage folks when we ourselves were facing the fight of our lives.

Diary entry: March 9, 2018

"Our nurse just prayed with us while we're waiting for Todd to go into surgery. This is literally the best hospital, and we are so thankful that we are in good hands. Keep praying.

Todd McGuire

"Gods got this   Todd's out of surgery. Surgeon said all went well. He's in recovery Keep those prayers coming Todd is currently undergoing his first treatment for GBS. called Plasmapheresis plasma exchange . He will have a 2-hour treatment   every other day for a total of 5 treatments. So. at the moment. we know we will be hospitalized for at minimum. 10 more days. Please continue the prayers "

People needed to know what we were going through, not because I was looking for sympathy. On the contrary, I wanted the public to be able to see that the God I serve is the real deal! I wanted the public to see a miracle in the making. That was our motive, and that's what we thrive on. Let God show up and show off!

Our wonderful OR staff were extremely pleasant, and we had the charge nurse lay hands and pray for us as I was heading into surgery. It was after that, when they were wheeling me in, that I jokingly said, "Please don't give me a hysterectomy!" As they shifted me from the gurney to the OR table, I felt the cool air in the room and the cold table below me. My arms were outstretched and the anesthesiologist began the process of putting me under. "Todd, count backward from 10," they said. 10-9-8-7....

I awoke with an after-market body part sticking out of the right side of my chest. Was this my chance to get well again? What are they going to do with this? I've never had dialysis. Is it going to hurt? I was about to find out that afternoon.

That night I felt the paralysis, almost as if it were spiders crawling up my belly. I knew from my medical training that if the paralysis reached my diaphragm, I could stop breathing. My breaths were already shallow, and I couldn't draw a deep breath. Chris had stayed the night (Penny had gone back to

ORDER MY STEPS

the trailer to get some much-needed sleep), and he asked me, "Dad, are you ok?" Not wanting to worry him, I said, "I'll be fine, son!" Under my breath, I began to call upon the name of Jesus. I literally prayed all night that I wouldn't lose my ability to breathe on my own, and thankfully, the Lord heard and answered my prayers! It moved up my chest, to just below my neck, and although I wasn't out of the woods, I was in a better place in my mind.

Chapter 9
Fear Is A Liar

Diary entry: March 10, 2018

"Please pray for Todd. He's certainly not used to laying down all the time and it's very hard on him in all ways. He's quite uncomfortable this morning...."

I had my first panic attack that day. This predicament of not being able to get out of bed and being a fall risk, had me feeling claustrophobic. Penny had experienced a few panic attacks and was claustrophobic, but this was a whole new ballgame for me! I had never been confined to a bed before, without being able to get out of it and go do what I wanted or needed to do. It took Penny and a nurse coming in, who also prayed with me, before I began to somewhat calm down. I just had to put my feet on the floor, even though they really didn't want me to. This was one of the hardest parts of this trial. Many times, Penny had to talk me down when I was panicking.

They moved me down to the ICU for more one on one care. The nursing staff did a great job taking care of me! Later that morning, they got everything set up to begin dialysis. The doctors had ordered 5 rounds, 1 every other day. I had trouble with my speech and my brain got a little foggy. My legs were numb to my hips, and I began to feel nerve channel's in my torso, a loss of feeling.

The nurse explained to me what she was about to attempt. She would hook the tubes up to my chest catheter and the pump would pull out my blood and run it through the dialysis machine. It would then spin at 2000 RPMs and the old plasma in my blood would separate and be removed, and new synthetic plasma would be mixed back in and be pumped back into my body. That's medical technology at its finest!

All of this would take about 3-5 hours, and I could go about my normal activity until it was finished. I usually fell asleep or rested through it. When the treatment was over, I felt like I had run a marathon. I was absolutely exhausted! But I would go to sleep for a few hours and awake feeling refreshed. The technician giving me the treatment said it would take at least 3 treatments before I started to feel better, or even stronger. A simple glass of milk was one of the things that helped my stomach feel better when I was receiving these plasma treatments.

Chapter 10
You've Got To Go Down Before You Can Go Up

Diary entry: March 11, 2018

"Todd had his second treatment today. They told him that he would feel like he ran a marathon, which he does, thus his visitors have been limited to 5 minutes. These treatments cause the virus to travel through the body to various locations, so today, he has Bell's Palsy and has lost use of his hands. They're treating him with steroids for the Bell's palsy. Please continue to hold us up in prayer. today Christopher spent the night with his Dad and I came home for a little sleep. We try to alternate so we can each have one night to get some rest. Christopher has been an absolute godsend in this whole ordeal. We know our daughter, Desiree, would be, as well, if she wasn't so far away. We are blessed with two wonderful children who have grown into awesome young adults and make us so proud. Have a great day, everyone, and hold your loved ones close."

Diary entry: March 13, 2018

"He's feeling very, very weak and tired after his 3rd treatment today and is trying to rest. On a positive note, both Todd I actually got sleep last night, the first sleep in 2 nights.

Todd McGuire

"We both feel a little more rested"

Over the next few days, treatments continued, and I was hoping to begin to feel better, but that wasn't happening. I was declining. I wasn't even allowed to sit on the edge of the bed, as I had no feeling in my lower extremities. Remember my pretty, yellow bracelet that they gave me? "Fall Risk!" I couldn't stop myself if I began to fall or even slide off the bed. I begged nurse after nurse to just sit me on the side of the bed and let my feet touch the floor. What a terrible feeling to be a full quadriplegic!

I had a wonderful physiotherapist who attended me, getting me to move my limbs. She recommended exercises for Penny to do with me throughout the days, to try and keep some of my strength, and try to regain some. I was so amped up to get better and get out of the hospital that, many times, I exercised my arms and hands too much and set myself back. This was a common thing throughout my hospital stays as I was very determined.

The days and nights began to run together now, and I was very uncomfortable. The staff brought me a new order of meds to try and keep me comfortable. I was prescribed a drug to help keep me calm and comfortable because I was hooked up to several leads for the monitoring units and I'd begun to feel claustrophobic and would wake up having panic attacks. Until you have an attack such as this, you have no idea how it feels! The staff tried to comfort me and continuously rolled me from side to side at my request, as I could not find a spot of comfort.

I normally used a CPAP Machine for sleep apnea, but I could not stand the mask on my face as it felt too claustrophobic. On one occasion, I looked at Penny and said, "Get that

ORDER MY STEPS

curling iron out of there!" Penny replied, "There's no curling iron, there, Todd." I was having pain of some type on my right thigh, and it literally felt like there was a hot, curling iron pressed up against my skin. Nerve pain is one of the very worst pains you could ever have, as I found that out through experience!

Chapter 11
Hallucinations

To top it all off, I began hallucinating as a result of some of the drugs they were giving me. I woke up one night and saw this woman at my bedside. I looked up at the ceiling and saw the dimmed lights. I recognized that I was in a hospital bed, however, I didn't know why I was there. I wasn't sure if I was in a hospital or a nursing home. I wasn't sure whether I was young or old. Where's my family? I wondered. I finally resigned myself to the fact that I was an old man in a nursing home and this lady beside me was my palliative care nurse. When she saw that I was bothered and awake, she said, "Can I get something for you, Todd?" I awkwardly looked at her, and said, "Maybe a facecloth?" She jumped into action. I watched her as she walked by my bed and I said in my head, "At least she's a hot nurse!" She wiped my face, and I couldn't help but stare at her. I said, "Ma'am, can I ask you a question?" She replied, "Yes!" I continued, "Ma'am are we related?" "I am your wife," was her incredulous reply. I then came back to myself and realized what was happening. I then rehearsed the story to Penny, and we both had a little chuckle.

The hallucinations continued. One night, I got angry with Penny, and said, "Aren't you going to let me in?" She said, "Into where?" I said "That door!" "What door, Honey? We're in the hospital." "We are not," I replied. "We're at the racetrack at Daytona, and you won't let me in the door to watch the race!" I then came back to myself and realized it was the drugs talking. Again!

Another evening, I woke up after hearing music playing. (Penny kept gospel music playing softly.) I looked at Penny and knew I wasn't decent, and I said, "Are those people in our room?" "What people?" she asked. "The Roark's? Are they singing in our room?" "No," she said. "They're singing on your phone." Ugh! I did it again!
I was beginning to see people when I closed my eyes, and they would snicker at me and point fingers in my direction. The only relief I got was when I stayed awake, but I desperately needed rest! We both did.

Chapter 12
You're in trouble Mister!

Shift change had taken place and a new set of nurses had been assigned. Our new nurse was a wonderful man, a retired US army veteran medic from West Virginia. He came in and we discussed my issues with hallucinations and sleeplessness. He said, "I've seen this before! You've been prescribed a PTSD drug, and we actually call it the suicide drug. It's not uncommon among military personnel to end their life while on this particular drug." I said, "I never want to take this again!!" He spoke with the doctor in charge, and they changed the drug. The new drug would come with its own issues, but it certainly made me feel better, and I could get some sleep! It was always a trial and error to what would work, as it is for any of us when we're receiving help from our health care providers.

Our nurse came in during the wee hours of Sunday morning to readminister the new drug, and I said, "You're in trouble, now, Mister!" He jokingly responded, "And, why is that?" I said, "Because I'm a preacher of the gospel and you've gotten me stoned on the Lord's day!" He and Penny got a great chuckle out of that! I then began to serenade him with the old John Denver song, "Country roads take me home," as I knew he was from West Virginia. In my inebriated state, I thought that it was a great gesture of thanks! I then looked at Penny, and said, "We can't tell anyone about this! We may never get another booking anywhere! People will be upset!!" She again got a great chuckle!

One of the great blessings of this whole journey was that I never lost my ability to speak, although it was mighty garbled at times, and I held on to my sense of humor. Laughter has always been a very important part of my existence and this whole trial was no exception! Penny and I had many laughs and chuckles throughout it all!

Chapter 13
I'm A Human Pincushion

Diary entry: March 20, 2018

"While driving our van home, Chris, Dave & Judy stopped for lunch at a Chick Fil A in Salem, Virginia. We had met Elona & Jason back when they came to N.B. to minister at Bannon Camp. She just happens to be the manager at this particular location and also just happened to be working out front today instead of back at the take-out window. She saw Chris and came out and greeted them all. She bought all their meals and told them she is praying for our family. What a blessing she was; truly love in action. May God bless this precious couple richly"

By now I had settled into a normal hospital routine. I received treatments every other day and blood work every morning. My fingers were so sore from being poked 3 times a day to test my sugar. I'd never had to have insulin, only a pill for my diabetes, so when they gave me insulin, it made my lips numb and I felt faint at times. They poked and prodded me until it seemed they couldn't poke anymore! I couldn't move anything and I slipped further into the helpless state of full care. Penny remained by my side, and the comfort I received from just knowing that she was there was priceless.

Todd McGuire

My parents came down to be with us and helped decide our next steps. Penny and my Doctors talked to the company that we had our travelers insurance through. They hoped to book me a special life flight back to Canada. Although this was happening all around me, I had not given up the fight, nor had I wanted to give up. As a matter of fact, it's caused me to fight harder than ever before! All I wanted was to be back home in Canada, surrounded by family and friends. This saga could not be over soon enough!

Diary entrance: March 23, 2018

"Because our being taken back to Canada is taking so long, our good doctors here in Zephyrhills have decided to start a 2nd round of plasmapheresis. Todd had his 1st of 5 more rounds yesterday, and it really made him feel stronger. We are so pleased with the care here and have decided that this is where God wants us until He decides it's time for us to leave. God has sent a few encouraging encounters here in the hospital. today I had a lady chaplain pray for me in the stairwell and encourage my heart. There's always a bright spot in every day. We are getting the best of the best of care and have submitted ourselves to the trial. If God has brought us to it, He surely will bring us through it, and all the glory will go to Him. Sure, we'd love to be closer to our family & friends, but for the time being, your prayers, messages of encouragement & gifts of financial blessings are ensuring we are not alone. We are in this together, just like one big family. We love you all & pray God's blessings upon you. You are part of our miracle & our testimony."

Chapter 14
New Beginnings

We received a visit from Pastor Phillip Johnson who has a church about an hour or so away. He was perusing social media over his dinner and saw a post from a mutual friend of ours, and God spoke to him to come and pray for me. He got up immediately and made the trip to my room at the hospital. I'm thankful for men and women who don't just hear the voice of God but respond to His voice! We had a prayer meeting that night. He said, "This is day 8. Do you know what Is significant about the number 8?" He went on to say that day 7 of creation is the day that God rested, but the next day was the 8th day, and it represented new beginnings. He prophesied right there, and said, "This is your day of new beginnings!" What an encouragement Brother Johnson was to us! He certainly was a very bright light in a dark situation!

Later that night when it was just Penny and me in the room, we were both praying and seeking God. We had a preaching video playing in the background. My wife was behind me, in intercessory prayer, and that's when I saw it: Angels! There were angels in our room! I could see them with my own eyes. They were swooping down, over my body, and I could feel a breeze from their flight. But there was one angel that sat in the upper, right-hand corner of the room. He wasn't the same color white as the other angels. He was an off white color, and he was looking at me with his arms folded and with a look of disdain on his face. I immediately recognized this angel for what it was: not a good angel, but a fallen. It was the spirit of infirmity. I called it out and got its attention. I proclaimed, "Spirit of infirmity; I recognize you, and I rebuke you in the name of Jesus Christ! Go back to the pit and report to your master and tell him that you've failed again!" When I looked again, he was gone. That's when the other angels recognized that I could see them, and there began a flurry of activity! The angels were swooping and flying around the room in a great flurry. What a beautiful scene! As I said earlier, I am not one that normally can see into the realm that is all around us. If only our eyes could be opened so that we could see this battle that wages around us, unseen! I knew that God had us in his hands and was not about to drop us!

Diary entry: March 22, 2018

"We still can't complain We have had so many wonderful people stop by to encourage us and to pray for us..... We are blessed Todd is commencing treatment 6 today of plasmapheresis plasma exchange. The Doctors. Nurses staff at this hospital are second to none When Todd got done with his therapy with one of his therapists. yesterday. she put her hand on his head and prayed for God to heal him. This blows our minds We are too blessed to be stressed and in the center of God's will. God has been so good to us"

Chapter 15
I've Refired

A few nights later, I was praying, as was Penny. We certainly had lots to storm Heaven about! We were settling down for bed, and Penny was puttering around our room. I was laying there, taking inventory of my body. Could I feel anything new? Has anything changed since the day before? Then, all of a sudden, like a bolt of lightning—from my cranium to my toes and out the ends of my feet, up and out of my arms and finger tips and then back up to my cranium—I felt this sensation! I hadn't felt anything, now, for almost 3 weeks, and right out of the blue, I began to experience some feeling. I worshiped and thanked God for about a half hour, and then without warning, pain! Pain like I had never experienced in my life.

Diary entry: March 24, 2018

"Todd got his 7th plasmapheresis treatment this morning. As per normal, he felt wiped out after his treatment. Add to that the added bonus that Todd's nerves are beginning to re-fire and he's had some pretty severe nerve pain, beginning last night. We are grateful for pain management that is available to keep Todd comfortable while his body heals."

We called for our nurse, whose name was Chris. He came in and I explained to him what I felt, and he said that this is a good thing! He sat down and helped put it into layman's terms. He said, "Imagine a big old factory that has been shut down for years. You are the key holder, and you fire that old factory back up. It's going to take some time for everything to get working and moving again." He continued, "Your body just refired!" Wow! What a feeling! My body just refired! I know I have a whole new level of gratitude and thanks for the prayers of the people of God, from around the world!

With this refiring also came a new set of hurdles and obstacles, namely, nerve pain. The pain felt like someone was shoving a hot knife into my hands and feet. Nothing else seemed to be affected, only my hands and feet. The pain got increasingly worse. After a couple of days of this, I remember praying, "Lord, I don't mind having to go through this, if it's Your will, but please take away the pain!!" I begged Him to remove the worst pain I had ever felt in my life.

Looking back on it, now I realize that pain is just part of the process. Just like the clay on the Potter's wheel. If it had feelings and could speak, it would ask the potter to not twist and hit it so. But, in order for the clay to become a beautiful object, there is a process of crushing, mashing and molding. Being molded is not comfortable, but when we ask for God to make us what He would have us to be, He takes that prayer seriously. In the process of being worked on, we may experience pain and uncomfortable trials, but as that old chorus says, "these trials have come to make us strong, though we don't see how they could." Truly, If I would've had a choice regarding whether or not I entered into this trial, I would've checked "no," but God knows what we need and when we need it!

ORDER MY STEPS

Diary entry: March 26, 2018

"Treatment 8 is completed. They are keeping Todd comfortable with pain meds. He started having severe nerve pain in his calves, feet, hands, last night. This is all to be expected as his nerves start to come alive. Please pray for as much pain-free rest as possible. It's hard to see your best friend in pain. He's called on the name of Jesus many, many times over these days, nights. We know our hope is in Him. He is our Refuge in the time of storm. We love you all and cannot tell you what all of your support means to us. You are so crucial to the healing process through your love and support during this season of our lives."

Chapter 16
I Want To Go Home

Dr. Khan, came back about day 17. He had been away for a week or so and we were still waiting for a response from the insurance company about our life flight. He asked the charge nurse when I was extubated (removal of a breathing tube). The nurse replied that I was never intubated. My neurologist was in shock. He said, "In all my 27 years of seeing this condition, you are the first that I've seen that was so severe but did not need to be intubated!" That's what my God can do, folks!

He made a few phone calls and set up a flight home. I was still doing my Plasmapheresis treatments and was heading into Round 8 when he announced that the last 2 rounds would be completed at the regional hospital in St. John, N.B, Canada. I would've jumped up out of that bed if I could've, but all I would've done would have been to fall on the floor. I was so thankful to be going home!!

My parents had flown down, and we had a chance to celebrate my mom's 60th birthday, in the hospital. Family is my heartbeat, and anytime we can be together we have fun and make the best of it! If anyone knows my dad, he can't sit still for very long. The man is a worker and has installed that work ethic within my sister and me. He and my son came up with a plan to drive our van back to Canada. We thought

Todd McGuire

I was going home a week earlier, so they left so that they could meet us back on home soil.

The wheels of justice turn slowly, but the wheels of this insurance company seemed to turn even slower. We soon found out what the big holdup had been. They had not recalibrated my hospital bed and did not have my proper weight, so they had me at about 150-200 pounds heavier than what I actually was! They thought that they would need a special plane to fly me home and were even saying that Penny might not be able to fly home with me, but at this time our van was already back safely home. Needless to say, once they got my proper weight, things began to fall into place quickly for the flight home, and we were relieved and thankful!

Let me say this, please. Purchase travel insurance before you journey anywhere! It's not safe to risk it. For example, the 3-hour flight that took me home cost $14,000.00. That's not including the price of my hospital stay, the meds that they administered, all my plasmapheresis treatments, etc. I had a bracelet on with a bar code, and every time I needed something, they would scan my wrist. I have an itemized list of meds and such that we received later in the mail, with my charts. It was astronomical!

Chapter 17
Fly Day

Diary entry: March 27, 2018

"The flight nurse was just here and we are flying tomorrow for sure. We'll be leaving from the Zephyrhills airport heading to Saint John, NB

Twenty-one days into my GBS journey and we're finally getting to return home! The Zephyrhills Fire and Ambulance service were dispatched to help transport me to—and onto—the plane. The aircraft was a late 70s model, Leer Jet. I'd never traveled in a luxury airliner before, and now I see why. Have you ever travelled at 30,000 feet, at 365 miles per hour, in a cigar tube? I have, and it was awesome!

The flight nurses were absolutely amazing and extremely helpful. They attended to my every need. Best of all, Penny traveled with me. Halfway through the flight, I began to feel pain in my right hip as the stretcher I was strapped to was not wide enough. I began to get more agitated but didn't want to say anything. When I could take no more, I mentioned my discomfort and the nurses immediately jumped into attention. One of them asked me if I wanted a little something to relax me and help with the pain. I said, "You can do that?" He then opened his "candy bag," as he called it. He drew up a syringe of clear liquid. He said, "This will take care of the pain for you!" He administered the drug through my PICC line and said, "You're going to feel this in 3, 2," and I said, "1!" It was wonderful to feel the pain leave. I calmed down and rested much better.

Diary entry: March 28, 2018

"We're back in Canada Robert Glenn were our incredible flight nurses"

When we finally touched down at the Saint-John airport, my heart leaped! When we disembarked from the plane, they had to sit my stretcher down on the tarmac until we got clearance from Customs and the tower to be loaded into the ambulance. It was cold. There were flurries in the air and ice on the tarmac. It was beautiful! I remember taking my hand, and with what little strength I had, I got my fingers to touch the cold pavement, and I thanked Jesus that I was home. There truly is no place like home! The local medics from Ambulance NB, loaded me into the ambulance and transported me to the Regional Hospital where I would finish my last 2 prescribed rounds of plasmapheresis.

Diary entry: March 30, 2018:

"Todd had his 10th and final plasmapheresis treatment. this morning He's feeling very tired exhausted as per always. with this treatment. He's sleeping soundly at the moment. Todd's pain is being managed. for the most part. They are saying that he will receive a nerve conductivity test. sometime. the first part of next week. They also mentioned that they would endeavor to transfer Todd to the Stan Cassidy Rehabilitation Centre. in Fredericton. in the near future. although no date has yet been given."

Chapter 18
I'm So Glad To Be In Canada

We arrived in St. John just before the Easter of 2018. I was quite a novelty, as I was "that patient with GBS that had flown in from Florida." I made a great guinea pig for the medical students, as the University is right next door. If I saw one student, I saw 15, and they all asked me the same thing every time. They wanted me to follow their finger with my eyes and many other questions and queries. They quickly played me out, although I wanted to be as helpful as possible. I finished my last 2 treatments at the hospital in the next couple of days.

When we arrived there, and folks heard that we were there, we came back from some procedure and there were homemade goodies in the room, cards, gift cards, flowers, etc. We were back with our people, and we were very grateful!! New Brunswick hospitality is amazing! We found out that we have more friends than we ever realized! I was also excited to get back and have a Tim Horton's coffee. I couldn't drink it all but what a treat!! I was going to wait to have another coffee for when I could lift it up and drink it myself. It's just not the same when someone else holds the cup for you, and you drink it through a straw.

Todd McGuire

Diary enrtry: April 1, 2018

"As you can imagine, this has been the most unique Easter we've ever celebrated, but it was great in its own way. First of all, they seemed to have gotten the knack for Todd's pain meds and so last night's sleep was very good for both of us. Then, we had a few special Easter miracles: Todd has gotten more movement in his arms, the feeling's coming back in his lower back spine, his hands are more open, he was able to wiggle his big toes, yesterday, ever so slightly, and for the coup de grace, he was partially able to shave himself for the first time today in over 25 days. In the midst of our day, we have also enjoyed 2 wonderful Easter services, online. We long to be physically present in church, but for now, this is the next best option."

Chapter 19
Longing For Normalcy

I would look out the window, overlooking the parking lot and see people going back to their lives, and I would ask myself; "Will I ever be able to do that again?" I would see our van parked across the way and wonder, would I ever get back in that, or even drive again?

Easter Monday I got incredible news. There was a bed open in the Fredericton hospital, and the next day they were going to transfer me to the Dr. Everette Chalmers Hospital. By now, bell's palsy had also set into my face. I had double vision, and my speech was slurred. I sounded kinda odd when I spoke, but I was home!

We did several videos of our journey to this point, and we kept the general public updated as much as we could through social media. I was becoming increasingly exhausted by the day. My body was fighting for its life, one heartbeat at a time. We kept negative thoughts and talks away from us. I didn't want to know the statistics about GBS! What I had heard was enough to discourage a healthy individual, let alone a sick one. Having and keeping a positive mindset is so important in life, even if you're not battling a sickness. You are what you think!

Not long after we arrived in St. John, I developed pain in my left leg. My leg also was visibly swollen and larger than my right leg. They took me for an ultrasound and found that I had developed a blood clot in my leg. I was placed on blood thinners, which was yet another scary result of constantly being in bed.

Diary entry: April 3, 2018

"We arrived back in Fredericton. NB. Todd was taken from the SJR to the DECH."

Tuesday came like a whirlwind. I was taken down to an ambulance, and we were transferred to Fredericton. I spent the first day and night in a ward with three other gentlemen. As always, Penny was right by my side. She slept in the crowded space on a reclining chair. Needless to say, it wasn't very comfortable, and we had had quite a few friends into see us that first day, so our wonderful doctor, Dr. Mafud, whispered into Todd's ear that he was going to get us into a private room, and early that second day we were moved into a room almost right across the hallway where we once again had our privacy. Thank you Jesus! When you consider forty days in a hospital and seven months at a rehab facility, it's a great blessing that we only had to spend one night in a ward with other people. God's favor shone on us throughout those eight months!

I got to spend the next thirteen days on the third floor of the Dr. Everett Chalmers Hospital, in the east wing. I got along with all my new nurses, and we began to cultivate relationships. Let me pause here for a moment, to say that, until you've had somebody have to do all your personal care, you haven't lived! My nursing staff had to do everything for me, as I could not do one thing for myself. I couldn't even keep my eyes shut when I slept, due to my facial

ORDER MY STEPS

paralysis, so Penny went and bought me a sleep mask at our local dollarama. One afternoon I was having a sleep with this sleep mask on, when a knock came to our door. Penny said my name and I awoke from my slumber to see nothing but darkness. I hollered, "Penny, I'm blind," as I moved my head from side to side, looking for light. After all I had been through, it wouldn't have surprised me if I did temporarily lose my sight. Penny began to laugh, which I thought was rude. She then came over and removed my sleep mask; it was a miracle! I could see again! We then both had a good laugh over this.

Diary entry: April 4, 2018

"Todd's first time sitting up in a chair in 28 days."

Chapter 20
Setback

We had a flood of visitors the first few days at the DECH, so much so that between us and our nurses, we decided to limit visitors and the length of their visits. One of our nurses had a husband who had also gone through GBS, and she was invaluable to us. I was exhausted! Each time folks came by, I wanted to see them and tell my story; however, it set me back about a week or more in my recovery. I couldn't' even do my physio exercises. A five-minute rule was implemented, and they put a note on our door to see the nursing staff before entering our room. The flow of visitors was then controlled. Our nurses became our protectors! We had developed so much more respect for nurses! They truly are the front line in health care and are so very vital!

I began to take a downturn in my health, and I finally hit rock bottom. Let me say this, though, "I've been to the bottom, and at the bottom, I found a Rock, and his name is Jesus!" When you're at the bottom, there is no place to go but up! We had a difficult road ahead, as my recovery would be a long, arduous process. In the middle of a calamity, you need to be looking for the light at the end of the tunnel and hope it's not an oncoming train!

We tried to have some fun as well through the pain. Sometimes I would ring my call bell, and when the clerk would come on the intercom, if I recognized the voice, I would then ask for a big mac and an order of fries. That always brought laughter! You need to learn how to have fun or even just a good laugh in any struggle. It's very much human nature to be negative, but laughter is like a medicine and needs to be administered, daily!

> "A happy heart is good medicine and a joyful mind causes healing, but a broken spirit dries up the bones."
>
> Proverbs 17:22 AMP

Diary entry: April 9, 2018

> "Todd has had a few little setbacks in strength and his double vision is back. We have had to reduce visiting hours as we were inundated with visitors when we arrived in Fredericton which had a negative effect on Todd. He couldn't do his therapies for a couple of days because of being so worn out from company. Todd's barber when we lived in Harvey, Jennifer, came all the way in to cut Todd's hair; his first haircut in over a month. She was so kind to do this for him. It was hard for Todd to sit up in a chair for her to cut his hair. He tires extremely quickly."

While I was at the DECH, our physiotherapist was trying to get me to sit up in a wheelchair. It was a very difficult process as I couldn't sit up for very long and got very uncomfortable quickly! They would place me in a sling and maneuver me over into the wheelchair. It took pillows under my feet and tilting me this way and that way as they tried to make it as comfortable as possible. When I was tired, I would get white and feel like I was going to pass out. This GBS zaps your energy, and you don't have very much to give.

ORDER MY STEPS

One night when my parents were visiting, the nurses got me into my wheelchair, and my parents wheeled me around out through the halls. It was really nice to get out of my room for the first time!

While I was at the DECH, I was also in desperate need of a haircut! It had been well over a month, and I couldn't stand the feeling of my hair being so shaggy anymore. Penny got ahold of my barber that I had out in Harvey, and Jennifer kindly came into the hospital and gave me a complimentary haircut. It was all I could do to sit up in a chair, while she cut my hair, but we were so grateful to Jennifer for her kindness to me! It's in the darkest times of your life that you get to see the goodness of others! We have been so blessed by so many people!

Chapter 21
My Smile Is Gone

It was very odd for Penny and others to no longer see a smile on my face! It was the first thing that most folks saw when they visited, and to not have it was certainly strange. I never lost my joy though, or my sense of humor. Penny says that it was one of the biggest things that kept her going! Penny and I would joke, and when I would laugh, it sounded fake, because of how my voice was, and my sound didn't match my facial expression, but we still laughed together. One night I was talking funny because of the drugs they were giving me for pain, and Penny took to laughing and laid right across my chest as she heaved with laughter. We had God and each other, and we were going through this trial together! True love is a beautiful thing!

April 6, 2018: Diary entry

"Todd had first EMG. Very discouraging. Nerves and muscles have no activity registered. Todd has upset fears he won't be able to walk again. Also. was supposed to get his direct line out but couldn't because of blood thinners for DVT Blood Clot in his left leg."

I was booked for my first nerve conductivity test (EMG), with Dr. Shafiq, on April 6th. They wheeled me down and all kinds of electrodes were attached to my arms and legs, and then they placed some needles into my muscles to evaluate electrical signals. The results were highly disappointing and discouraging to the point that Penny did not update our Facebook page about it. The results were written across our neurologist's face. It was a terrible result! There was hardly any electrical activity going on within my muscles. They wheeled me back up to my room. The RN assigned to me for this shift was amazing! She did damage control and talked me "down off the wall," so to speak. She told us that it was expected for the first EMG to be this way, especially with a case of GBS as bad as mine. I determined again that I was going to fight with everything in me to beat this!

Chapter 22
Heavenly IVIG

Diary entry: April 10, 2018

"Todd started IVIG treatments today. He will have one a day for 5 days"

Around this time, it was determined that I should begin Intravenous Immunoglobulin Therapy (IVIG). So, on April 10th, I began IVIG treatments in my room. I would have one a day for five days. We prayed that as the IVIG treatments would flow into my body that God would send down His heavenly IVIG as well, and heal me completely. That I would come out of this sickness, healthier than I had been before GBS struck!

What is in the immunoglobulin? Immunoglobulin is made from donated blood plasma. During manufacture, everything except a type of immunoglobulin called IgG is removed from the plasma. IgG is very good at fighting bacteria and viruses. IgG has other effects too, so it isn't just used for people with immune deficiency. You might hear about immunoglobulin being used in some people with other immune (autoimmune) problems.

About an hour into my treatments, I would feel this sudden energy boost. It wasn't like a caffeine high after coffee, or

Todd McGuire

a sugar high, but I felt more like Popeye when he took his spinach. It was incredible! I really started to notice and feel a positive difference with the IVIG treatments! We were blessed to have the best of care from Florida back to New Brunswick!

The nursing department and staff were my saving grace! "Thank you 3 East, for your care and concern! When anxiety is high, a good hug or a laugh, and easy talk, helps to relieve it every time." We love our Nurses!

Chapter 23
Moving Day

From the beginning of our journey, now forty days in, I said repeatedly to doctors, nurses, and specialists, that I needed to get to the Stan Cassidy Centre for Rehabilitation (SCCR) in our Capital city of Fredericton, New Brunswick, Canada. Well, finally, moving day arrived! Another new journey! Another chance to meet some absolutely incredible staff and make more long-lasting friendships. I was nervous and joyous at the same time, after all, I was leaving my comfort zone that we'd lived in for a couple of weeks, and we were now going to another new normal.

Dr. O'Connell, who would be our doctor at the Stan Cassidy, had come to visit me a few days before I was transferred over. She told us how that when we moved over to the rehabilitation centre that I would have to be dressed. No more hospital gowns! I hadn't had real clothes on for forty days! SCCR is not a hospital but a rehab and that's reinforced by the clothing rule. It would be time for me to get to work so I could walk again! It would be intense as I work hard to get better! Dr. Michael Hader signed my release and stated that my body was now free and clear of any viruses and ready to move.

You may wonder why at times I say, "our journey" or "our lives," always speaking as if I was not alone in this journey, for in fact, I was never alone on this journey. My beautiful Penelope had never left my side. She had slept in chairs, on cots, on couches and used staff showers, ate hospital food, and watched me become a shell of my former, strong self. If anybody on this journey was deserving of a handclap and praise, it was her. I owe a ton of credit to my incredible wife! Staff from every hospital had seen her unfailing love for me and had respected that. In fact, when the doctor came in to release me to the SCCR, he wrote on the bottom of his notes, that, "These two come as a package deal." I love you, Penelope! Thank you for being you!

I still had those same questions haunting my mind: Would I ever walk again? Would I be ready for this next stage of our journey? Will things ever be the way they used to be? Am I going to be ok? Then, I met the first point of contact from the Stan Cassidy Centre for Rehabilitation: Denis and Linda! They brought with them the weight, clout, and knowledge of the SCCR. They were, and are, incredible representatives and ambassadors for the centre.

The hospital and the rehabilitation centre were connected by a pedway, so it was not a long journey at all! Denis loves to joke, so, we laughed and talked the whole way over! Denis was our tour guide as they wheeled me along. What a fun guy!

As we made our way through the pedway and into my new temporary home, I wondered, "Was I really ready?" I had so many questions. I couldn't move any part of my body from my neck down, and I had Bell's palsy and double vision. I thought, I must be a cute sight to see. Welcome to the nut house, one-eyed Willie!" I hoped that this wouldn't be like the song, Hotel California, where you can check in but never leave! I was ready to be home but that was a futile thought, at least for the time. As it is with facility change and meeting new staff, my anxiety was high, however, I was ready for this new chapter!

We made it to room 109, where we would live for seven months. This was the place where I would begin to get better! My recovery would be slow but at least I had arrived where I wanted to be from day one! Welcome to SCCR!

Let me give you a quick history on the SCCR. This information is taken directly from their website:

"To those who live in Fredericton or who have visited the SCCR, "Stan Cassidy" is recognized not only as a man's name, but as a symbol of the dedication and innovation which resulted in the establishment itself. Stan Cassidy was an engineer who was born and raised in Fredericton. With a Master's Degree in Electrical Engineering and a Doctor of Laws Degree, Mr. Cassidy was an enterprising and lively businessman who passionately wanted to help individuals with special needs of New Brunswick play a meaningful role in society. He recognized that the lack of rehabilitation facilities east of Montreal was an obstacle for many of these people and took the initiative to change it.

In 1957, Mr. Cassidy brought a plan to the NB Minister of Health and Social Services and within less than a year and a half the doors of the Forest Hill Rehabilitation Centre were officially opened. After his death in 1993, the Forest Hill Rehabilitation Centre was renamed the Stan Cassidy Centre for Rehabilitation in honour of Mr. Cassidy and the impact he had on rehabilitation services in New Brunswick.

In 2006, a new neurological rehabilitation facility was built directly beside the Dr. Everett Chalmer's Hospital. This facility proudly took on the name "Stan Cassidy Centre for Rehabilitation," along with the mandate to deliver neurological rehabilitation across the province of New Brunswick.

Diary entry: April 16, 2018

"We arrived at the Stan Cassidy Centre for Rehabilitation. Todd was excited to be dressed in real clothes for the first time in 40 days. There are no johnnies hospital gowns at the SCCR."

Chapter 24
I'm Finally Here!

As they brought me into my room, I began to take inventory of our new accommodations. It was a private room, with a large window to the right, overlooking the parking lot. I could also see the Department of Transportation school bus garage, which brought a sense of familiarity, as I drove a school bus, previously, and I had been to that particular garage several times.

I could see a cot set up for Penny, for which we both breathed a huge sigh of relief. We were told that they encouraged a family member staying, as it helped the patient recover more quickly.

As I looked up, I saw a track on the ceiling that looked like it went into the restroom. As I looked to the left, I saw a toilet: a real toilet! As Denis was getting things set up, I asked him if I was allowed to use that toilet. He said, "Yes, of course!" I was so excited that I could actually get lifted to an upright position to do my business. After all, if you have ever spent anytime bedridden, then you can appreciate how awful it is to try to use a bedpan, especially for someone who is the size of a small quarter ton truck, like me. Bedpans and I do not mix! On a positive note, I'm glad that I had never become incontinent. Thankfully, I never lost any of my feeling to go to the bathroom throughout the whole journey, and I never had to have a catheter. That was a blessing!

I asked Denis if I could go to the toilet. He brought out the sling and lift from the ceiling, and he hoisted me into the air. My next stop was the flush. When I landed safely, tears began to well up in my eyes, and I broke down and sobbed. Denis came over quickly and gave me a huge hug and said, "Through this journey, your dignity has been stolen. Today is the day you begin to get it back!" That meant more then he will ever know, after all, my dignity had been stolen! No one ever wants to be in a position where someone else has to do everything for them, and I mean everything. Toilet duty was not a good time for me, or anyone, I'm sure, in this position. I had gone from being fully independent to being totally dependent on someone else. Unless you have been in that position, you will never know the psychological impact it has on you. I somehow needed to muster up enough strength to get through this and press on, and that I did. Today would be the beginning of my comeback!

As the day went on, other staff began to stop by, and all of them seemed to have an incredibly, awesome disposition. We slowly began to get to know them all as the days progressed, and what a thrill it was!

We had a chance to meet the team assigned to us:
- Dr. Colleen O'Connell, who, let me say, is the best doctor to ever grace the face of this earth. She is amazing!
- Christa, our physiotherapist, along with Sam and Celine, who were her assistants.
- Karen, who was our occupational therapist, with assistants, Jenny Lynne and Cameron.
- Keri, who was my speech therapist and assistant, Julie.

ORDER MY STEPS

- Beth, respiratory therapist.
- Dr. Becky Mills, psychologist.
- Sharon, clinical dietetics.
- Micheline, recreational therapy.

Everyone of them had to assess me to see at what level I was in my recovery. They gave me the rest of the week to settle in, slowly, and began our regime on Monday morning.

I stayed in bed the first few weeks but not by choice. My muscle mass had greatly diminished. I couldn't roll over by myself, move, or feel hardly any of my body, except the excruciating pain in my feet and hands. They prescribed some new meds for me, as well as Dilaudid, a pain medication. Whew! That was an amazing drug! 1mg every 3 hours, or PRN as needed. Calgon, take me away!

We had already seen many miracles since I first became ill:
1. I did not have to be intubated as the paralysis went over my diaphragm.
2. I've always been able to swallow, although initially I had a few small issues with it.
3. I've always been able to verbally communicate, although my speech has been quite garbled, at times.
4. I did not need to have a lumbar puncture to be diagnosed with GBS.
5. I didn't need to have a feeding tube, and I was able to eat the entire time, although, I didn't have much of an appetite for quite a while.
6. I've had no pressure sores or skin issues.
7. I've never had to use a catheter and have retained control of all my bodily functions.

We have certainly given thanks many times over the last two years and always will at the miracles we got to witness and be a part of. God is good, all the time!

Isn't it funny that when you have a painful spot on your body, it's almost like a beacon that is asking for people to touch that spot. Why is that? My feet hurt the worst of all, and when people came Into my room, they'd grab, squeeze, twist, and tap them to greet me! I would respond with an OUCH! I couldn't help it! I began to get PTSD about my feet being hurt, that I still have, even to this day.

Chapter 25
Check Your Privacy At The Door

Bathroom duty was the hardest. I never got used to others helping me with such a private duty. It wasn't long after I arrived at the Stan Cassidy that we had some nursing students assigned to us to complete their clinicals, internships, and get some practical, on-the-job training. It was 8:00 am and my regular nurse, Denis, brought in the student instructor, who immediately grabbed me by my feet. "OUCH!" Needless to say, it wasn't a great start to the day.

I asked Denis if I could go to the restroom before we started our day. He and this new person—invading my space—loaded me into the sling and lifted me to the toilet. It was just what I needed on a Monday morning: some person that you do not know looking at your hinder parts, while trying to make casual conversation with you! This was anything but casual! Eating nachos is casual. Going to the restroom in a lift is not casual.

I was asked if I minded if a student could shadow my nurse for a few hours. I didn't care, at the time, until after my restroom duty was done, and I was hoisted high into the air, to be cleaned up. That's when I minded. One student, eh? How about three staring at my under carriage in awe.

Todd McGuire

I've never had anybody ever look at my nether region with such anticipation. I was mortified! It's bad enough that the tissue was like 220 grit sandpaper. Now, I had what feels like someone with a palm sander buffing that baby to a shine! Ugh!! Once they'd done learning, I got hoisted to my bed to get ready. The students stand around looking at me. I'd not even had a coffee yet, and my space and body had been invaded.

Denis then wanted to slide me up higher into the bed, so he grabbed my left arm and reached to my right side and lifted. When he did that, pain shot through my left arm. "Ouch! You pinched my chicken wing!" By then I had had enough, and the onlookers all knew it. They all immediately evacuated the premises. Penny came to console me, and through angry, embarrassed tears, I said, "I can feel my arms! I guess It's going to be a good day after all!"

It was always all about finding the good part of everyday! Not every day was good, but there was good in every day, and we would find it, at all costs!

Chapter 26
Getting Into A New Routine

Our daily routine had been set. We had been at the SCCR for a few weeks, and we'd met most of the nurses as they worked shifts of four days on, four off. We had gotten to know our therapy teams and were working well with them. Every morning started between 8-8:30 for me. Penny usually got us both breakfast. An English muffin, with coffee, and maybe an egg. On Wednesday's, it was bacon day!! My dietician didn't like the fact that I ate 3-4 pieces once a week. She said, "It's 100 calories per slice," which after I googled and fact checked, I found out it was actually only 45-65 calories. I had lost a pound a day for 60 days, and it was my muscle mass which was greatly depleted. Now that I was in daily therapies, I was getting stronger and starting to feel my muscles come back, which was great!

I generally left the room for therapies around 9 or 9:30. At first, because of how acute my condition was, I could only do one physio session and maybe one occupational therapy session, and then I was completely wiped out! I would go back to my room and rest, and after dinner I would go to speech therapy and recreational therapy. At the beginning it was 2-3 therapies a day, then rest and recover. They had my rest times scheduled, as it is routine with any GBS patient in my condition. Fatigue was a big part of all this, and rest helped me recover my strength and get well.

Todd McGuire

I would bed down early in the evenings. Penny busied herself with writing thank you notes, visiting with people, and keeping everyone updated on social media. We had so many wonderful friends and family that wanted to visit with us. I remember one day we had twenty-seven people come by. At 4:00 in the afternoon I said to Penny, "I can't take anymore. I am exhausted." She had eleven more people come by that evening. The SCCR nursing staff had to put a stop to the consistent flow of people. They made it mandatory for everyone to check with the nursing station first! I'm so glad they had my back, as I could easily miss some therapies because of exhaustion.

On April 18th I was assigned to a power wheelchair which began to give me some independence. I couldn't feel my hands much yet, and I certainly couldn't run the chair at full capacity, but I could go a whopping 2.3 kms per hour! That was breakneck speed for me who had been in bed for 3 months. The loaner chair was at max width for most of the doors, and I had a screw sticking out of the right side about a quarter inch, and that was enough to catch on doorways, etc. Believe me, I caught a few! As a matter of fact, I could take you around and show you some of the "tatoos" that I left on the building. I actually ripped a whole piece of trim off one doorway while going into the gym. Shhhh... don't tell anybody.

One day we thought that we would take my newfound independence and go visit the nurses on 3 East, at the DECH, right next door. There was quite an incline on the sidewalk that took us over to the hospital. I somehow got off the sidewalk, into the grass. Penny was trying to "right" the wheelchair, which would have been impossible as the chair alone weighed around 400 pounds. She was praying out loud as I somehow finally got the chair out of the dirt

ORDER MY STEPS

by maneuvering around. Behind every successful man is a woman worrying and praying, a lot!

We finally managed to get up to the hospital safely and then took the elevator up to the third floor. I may have also left some dings and dents in that as my hands weren't fully working, so it was all trial and error. The nurses were all so glad to see us and see my progress. Throughout the time that we were staying at Stan Cassidy, I would go up different times and see all my nurses. We developed a bond with our dear caregivers that we have to this day.

The evenings now brought me a little more independence, and if I was up and felt like it, I could go outside and get some air, or roll around the empty hallways and think. My first time outdoors, since this whole debacle began, was in my power chair. What a joy to get outside and feel the wind and sun on my face! Oh, all the things we commonly take for granted!

Chapter 27
Anniversary Celebrations Institution Style

Diary entry: April 20, 2018

"Penny ordered a meal from the Diplomat. and we shared it for our anniversary meal. Todd received his new air mattress which is much better for him than the regular hospital mattress. It keeps him moving so that he won't get so sore Dr. O'Connell gave him 2 new pain meds for the nerve pain that he has. They have certainly helped"

"22 years ago today. we said our vows and promised to love one another in sickness and in health. poverty   wealth. etc.. and we meant every word   This is a first for us. as we are spending this anniversary at a rehabilitation centre. but at least we are together I love you. Todd.   always will We truly are better together Here's to many more happy years as Husband   wife "

All I wanted on our anniversary was to be able to take Penny out to eat, like we normally would've done! It was so hard on me, and this was the first time I really had a good cry about it. I cried for a good, what felt like, ten minutes, or so. Penny told me to let it all out. I felt much better after I let my emotions flow freely, and we made the

Todd McGuire

very best of this, our 22nd wedding anniversary.

Chapter 28
What Am I Doing In A Wheelchair?

I was traveling one night and I looked up at one of the dome mirrors in the hallway, and thought, Todd, what are you doing in a wheelchair? I guess the weight of the situation really began to hit me. I remained positive, though, and spoke back. "Because, it's my only mode of transportation until my legs are back." I spoke, thought, and stayed positive. GBS may have temporarily disabled me, but I would be back on my feet!

Diary entry: April 25, 2018

"Todd was able to stand with the aid of a stander and his therapists this afternoon. for the first time in 49 days They said that he did very well Sometimes. people even faint the first time....

Also. Todd was able to finally have his port taken out that was used for his plasma treatments. This was the third attempt. and it's finally gone
Thirdly. we found out yesterday that Todd has lost an additional 12 pounds. bringing him to only 40 pounds away from his goal weight "

Todd McGuire

My regular rehab doctor, Dr. Colleen O'Connell, went on a medical trip, and she had a colleague fill in for her. On his first visit, he told me that I only had a 13% chance of ever walking again. What a drag! "Not today, Satan; get thee behind me!" I never had him back again. I left strict orders with the nursing staff that unless I was dead on the floor, that I didn't need him. If I needed a doctor while mine was away, I would go wait in the ER at the DECH. No negativity allowed here!

Chapter 29
Finding The Silver Lining In Every Cloud

Diary entry: April 30, 2018

"Todd enjoyed some time in the stander, more time than last and also spent about 20 minutes with the passive bike. Everyone's amazed at how far Todd's come in the last 2 weeks. Please pray he continues to make great progress. We love you all."

Spring had arrived and was in full swing. The snow was gone, the sun was up longer, and the days were warm. We tried to find any reason to celebrate! Day 100 of being hospitalized, Penny made posters and put up balloons and streamers to celebrate. On Canada Day we put up Canada Day flags, streamers, etc. I even had a Canada flag on the back of my wheelchair. New-Brunswick Day, Acadian Day, Nurses Week, Therapist Week, Administrative Assistant Day, any birthdays, etc. We bought treats for our nursing staff and then for our therapy staff. We loved all our team and wanted them to know it! It was very important to us to keep maximum positivity and minimum negativity!

After I was done with therapies for the day, Penny and I could be found in Therapeutic Park. It was our beauty in an ugly situation.

Diary entry: May 2, 2018

"Pain is under control again. We have to pace each day accordingly as Todd can only spend 1 to 1.5 hours in his chair, max. Todd has scheduled rest periods each day, to recover between therapies. He has a speech pathologist, a physiotherapist, an occupational therapist, a recreational therapist, and a psychologist."

We watched the flowers bloom daily as the leaves began to sprout on the trees. Bushes and shrubs began to blossom, and I would sit in the sun and relax while Penny would quietly read. They have beautiful purple orchids in the park and a large variety of flowers.

This park is named so perfectly. Therapeutic Park, it truly is. There is a gazebo, water fountain, several shade trees, swings, and a jungle gym for the little ones that are here for their daily therapies, or for family that would come by to visit.

We would spend our evenings out there with other patients, as well. We have made lifelong friends and acquaintances because of that park. A few times, Penny brought her accordion out and we sang for the patients. Music and singing were also a very real part of my therapy as this is what we have always done!

Chapter 30
We Are Progressing!

Diary entry: May 8, 2018

Todd worked out on scifit. 1/2 mile. Wiped him out

Diary entry: May 16, 2018

Todd stood 3 times using parallel bars.

Diary entry: May 18, 2018

Todd picked up a guitar and strummed a few chords. Playing guitar will be part of his rehab.

Diary entry: May 21, 2018

Todd said I feel like I could lift my leg up and proceeded to do just that. He lifted his left knee way up off the bed.

Diary entry: May 29, 2018

Todd fully stood using wall bars.

Diary entry: May 30th

2nd Emg much better results than last time Dr. Shafiq

Todd McGuire

was pleased. All Todd's nerves are firing from his head to his toes. Upper body is mostly working as normal. Now to strengthen and work on the lower body. Todd's first day back on Facebook

Diary entry: May 31, 2018

Todd's personal best on scifit so far. 1 mile in 9 minutes. When he first started it took him 15 mins to do 1/4 mile.

GBS strikes everyone differently, but it generally is slow recovery. Someone gave GBS the acronym, "Getting better slowly," and that has certainly been my experience. The turtle is the national symbol for GBS. But never forget that between the turtle and the hare, the turtle won the race! Slow and steadily, I've gotten better!

This syndrome started in my feet, and it is what they call an ascending paralysis. The first place the virus attacks is your central nervous system. It then moves up your nerve channel's and stops when, and where, it wants. Though you can see similarities in GBS patients, it really is a case-by-case situation.

We have since met other GBS patients, and we always have an instant connection! It is said to be rare: 1/100,000 will become ill with this syndrome, they say. Also, the myelin sheath, the substance that covers the nerves, heals at a rate of a millimeter a day. It's a slow process, but I have steadily been healing. Even to this day, I am still experiencing healing in my body. Thank you, Jesus!

Guillain-Barré syndrome (GBS) is a rare condition in which a person's immune system attacks the peripheral nerves. People of all ages can be affected, but it is more common in

ORDER MY STEPS

adults and in males. Most people recover fully from even the most severe cases of Guillain-Barré syndrome.

For me, the paralysis travelled all the way to the top of my head, and the damage caused in my nerves was very extensive. I then had to take inventory, weekly, of my returning feelings and movement. It was a painfully, slow process, but we knew that because God had ordered my steps, all would be well. It may not be today, or tomorrow, but our trial did have an expiry date. We anxiously awaited that day!

> Diary entry: June 3, 2018
>
> *Todd rolled over by himself.*
>
> Diary entry: June 4, 2018
>
> *Todd was in a manual chair this morning to see how it is. He will eventually graduate to it.*

One would never know how it feels to go from a power chair, to a manual one, unless you have been there. That's part of the process of gaining back your independence. My arms were returning a little more every week. I had issues with my left hand being able to grip the wheel firmly, but it was a start. I would begin to leave the power chair and go in the manual one. It may have taken a little longer to get to where I was going, but I just had to plan accordingly. When you are trying to beat a syndrome like GBS, you need to have stubborn tenacity that breaks the barriers in front of you. You must kick yourself out of bed, although it would be easier to just stay there. God didn't design us to become stagnant. We must trudge forward, no matter how slowly. One moment, one step, one day at a time, in the face of the enemy and opposition. Press On! Don't quit!

Todd McGuire

Diary entry: June 10, 2018

Todd restrung his Taylor guitar

I created my own therapy one Saturday afternoon as I tried to restring my acoustic guitar. I couldn't feel my hands yet, and I had minimal movement. It took me two hours and a lot of effort, but I did it! Now it's time to practice.

Diary entry: June 14, 2018

Todd took his first steps on the parallel bars

Diary entry: June 17, 2018

Todd's pain has been lessening and his pain meds are all being reduced.

Diary entry: June 26, 2018

It took Todd 9 weeks to finish his first wooden sign in rec therapy. McGuire sign

Chapter 31
Cabbie Yoga

I found out that our local Maritime Gospel Music Association wanted to have a benefit concert for us. They would host this concert in our honor at a local church on Saturday, June 23rd. We were so thankful for their willingness to help and the folks that began to prepare to sing at it. Would this be my opportunity to get out of the rehab for the very first time? We were hoping that we could go to it.

I spoke with therapists, and they were all for it. A few days before the concert, our Recreational Therapist had booked the wheelchair accessible bus from SCCR, and we were going to do a dry run to make sure everything would go well the evening of the concert.

The bus arrived and the driver got out and lowered the gate for the ramp. I got on the ramp and up we went into the bus. As I got settled into my spot, our therapist and driver fastened my chair down. Front wheels and back wheels. They then made sure my lap belt was on. The last thing I ever wanted to do was fall out of my chair. The shoulder belt was also applied, and my chair brakes were locked. We were ready to go!

We made it to the venue, all in one piece! The elevator, at the church, worked perfectly, and I was stoked! I was so excited to get out to a wonderful concert and see the friends that had come out to support, even though I wasn't sure I'd last through the whole concert, due to fatigue. We finished our trial run and made it back to the SCCR, anticipating that Saturday evening!

Today was the day! A local Taxi company was booked. Penny helped me get all gussied up! I was now in a manual chair that I used most of the time, as my arms were recovering quite well. I could wheel the chair myself, and besides, it was great upper body exercise.

The taxi showed up on time. Penny and my mom had gone on ahead and set up our product table. Meanwhile, my dad stayed with me and was going to follow the taxi over to the venue in his own vehicle. The ramp was let down in the back of the late model dodge caravan, and then I was wheeled into place. I checked my lap belt, locked my wheels, and waited for the driver to lock down the chair into the straps. I felt him nudge my back wheels, and I assumed that he was hooking them up. Note to self..."Never assume anything when it comes to your own safety." He then reached through the doorway and fastened the front of my wheelchair down. I heard my father say to the driver; "Shouldn't you fasten the rear straps too?" The driver said, "No. He's got his lap belt on."

I had only been in a wheelchair accessible vehicle once, with a very competent staff. This driver should know what he's doing, right? Have you ever boarded an airplane and asked the pilots if they knew how to fly the plane? No. You just know that they're hired to fly this plane, so they must know what they're doing, right? So, even though this is not an airplane, and this guy is not a pilot, he should know the procedure when hooking up a wheelchair. Well, never

ORDER MY STEPS

assume anything!

The driver got in the front and radioed dispatch and told them that we were loaded and leaving for the destination. This ride was going to be $11.00 one way. We only had a $20 bill but didn't expect any change, as it was a tip.

We darted out the SCCR driveway and headed for the street. We turned onto Regent Street and headed down the hill. As we made the turn, I felt the chair kind of moving, but I thought maybe I was just being paranoid.
My dad was close behind us, and we headed for the light at the intersection of Regent and Montgomery Streets. The light had just changed to yellow, and the driver thought he'd have time to zip through it, so he gunned it. It changed to red, and he abruptly slammed on the brakes, and that's when it happened. Inertia!

I felt the chair going over frontwards. It all happened so fast but in a slow-motion kind of way. I remember thinking, this isn't going to be good! Halfway over, I looked out of the side window and realized, this is it! My worst fear is coming true! As I lunged forward, I tried to prevent the fall by grabbing the front seats and pushing against them, but my strength just wouldn't allow it.

The next thing I knew, I was face down on the floor of the taxi, with the wheelchair on top of me, pinning me down. And then PAIN! Oh, the pain! The driver asked, "What do I do?" And I screamed, "I don't know, but I can't stay here long!" He jumped out, opened the side door, and ran back to get my father, who was right behind us and saw this whole thing unfold.

The PAIN! My legs were being crushed, my back was

twisted, my feet were under the foot pegs of the wheelchair and twisted backwards. My left knee and right ankle were in excruciating pain! By now, Dad was at the other door, and I holler for him to get me out! "Get this chair off of me!" He said, "I'm trying Toddy!" A couple bystanders stopped to join the rescue efforts.

Let me just interject this here. "The Police, Fire, or Ambulance were never notified..." that should have been the first thing that the driver should have done or at least called his dispatch to do it for him.

I was being crushed under the wheelchair. My head was on the floor, up between the front seats, by the console. I tried to grab the front seat backs again, to help lift myself and to alleviate the pain, but to no avail. Dad and another man were in the back, and they tried to get the front straps loose. I remember saying, "Dad, my lap belt for the chair is hooked. You're going to have to unhook that first."

A lady jumped into the front of the taxi and told me to focus on her. I could tell that she had some sort of medical training as she ask me in a calm manner to focus, and she asked if I thought that anything was broken.

I was screaming like a little girl, at the top of my lungs, in pain. I began to black out, and she grabbed my attention, again. "Sir! Do you think anything is broken?" I said, "If anything, my left knee, if not broken, is certainly dislocated, and I'm pretty sure my right ankle is broken."

The team got the chair off me, and they reached under my arms, unfolded me, and laid me down on the floor of the taxi.

Let me say this: Pain will make you do and say a lot of things, and believe me, I was doing and saying!

ORDER MY STEPS

All I could think was, get me back to the SCCR: they'll know what to do! Still, no First Responders were called at all, and all I could think was what if my knee and or ankle is broken? I'll have to go back to the hospital until everything heals!

Then my anger turned to the incompetent driver. He's the one to blame! He never fastened down the back of my chair! If I have anything broken, or if this sets me back in anyway on my road to recovery, then it's this driver who is to blame as well as the taxi company!

He closed the doors, jumped back into the taxi, and radioed dispatch, telling them that he was returning to the SCCR. "The patient fell out of his chair!" Way to try to turn the tables and make yourself look innocent! He then spun around in the middle of the intersection and raced back to the rehab, like he was an ambulance.

I was still not buckled in or strapped down. This could've gone from bad to worse in a hurry! All the driver could say was, "Yup. It's those sudden fetch-ups that get you every time!" He said that 3 times, and I felt that if he said that once more, that I had a sudden fetch-up for him!

We arrived under the canopy of the rehabilitation entrance. Someone ran in to tell the security guard, and he notified the nursing staff, who came running out. I was still in excruciating pain in my thighs, knee, feet, and especially my right ankle. They had enough common sense to call 911, and an ambulance was dispatched. They arrived on scene in seconds. Between the nurses and medics, they put a plan in action to get me out.

The hole that I was in on the floor was not wide enough for a spine board, so they used a sheet to slide under me and pull me out. They finally get me onto the stretcher.

Meanwhile, Penny and Mom had been notified, and they arrived, hearing my screams from the taxi. They were both livid. Mom was so mad that she even punched the wall!
I thought, when this is over, we're all gonna need some saving.

The nurses administered 2 mg's of diloded to help alleviate the pain. One nurse spoke up, and said, "Todd, remember your 10 fingered prayer!" Through pain and a grimace, I asked, "What 10 fingered prayer?" She said; "I Can Do All Things Through Christ Who Strengthens Me." I thanked her and said, "You bring me the driver back here and I will show him the Five-Fold Ministry!"

By the time I was in the back of the ambulance, the meds had kicked in, and I had calmed down. My pain was at a manageable state. We arrived at the ER and went quickly in. My rehab doctor had been notified and she called the physician at the ER, gave him my history, and instructed him to take as many x-rays as was needed.

I was whisked away to the imaging department and had my knee and right ankle x-rayed from many angles. I was then taken to a room and waited to be seen by the doctor. I was still in an incredible amount of pain.

The nurse on duty asked where we were going, so we told her about the benefit concert that we had been on our way to, and that Penny and I were also singers. She asked if we would sing for her. We sung her the song that we had been practicing for the concert, and she cried. If no one else had been touched, at least that nurse from the ER was!

ORDER MY STEPS

The doctor came in and informed us that nothing was broken, to which we all thanked God! He said, "All you have is some very bad tissue damage that will heal in a few days." He also said, "As far as your legs, you got a stretch that you didn't want. Sir, you will be sore for a while!" And I was.
They wheeled me back through the breezeway to the SCCR and to my familiar room. My nurses were all glad to see me, and I was tuckered out from the whole episode. The next day was Sunday. It gave me a chance to rest. The ER doc was right: I was so sore!

Some of my family came over for a few hours, and we spent time visiting and rehashing the events of the evening before. Word of the incident had spread like wildfire among the SCCR staff, and by the time Monday morning rolled around, I was the talk of the facility. No patient had ever been upset in a taxicab, and the concerns began to mount. What if I had banged my head or gotten a neck or back injury? What if it had been a patient with a spinal cord injury? The therapists were very concerned, as they had every right to be. This taxi company was the one that our rehabilitation facility commonly recommended and called upon. Calls were made to the police, cab company, City of Fredericton, etc. Reports were made, and the incident was recorded for future use.

I believe I have started a new fad called Cabbie Yoga. Ouch! Don't try this at home!

Chapter 32
Celebrate Every Small Victory!

Diary entry: June 28, 2018

Todd did his second board transfer from the bed to the wheelchair and back and it went wonderfully. His first was on May 28th and was difficult. Todd no longer needs regular speech therapy as he has reached levels that Keri has never seen with any other patients.

Summer!

Summer arrived and my therapies were going great! I had so much more movement in my arms, and my feeling was just about back in my upper body. My legs were still weak, but at least I could feel them, and that gave me hope.

I began to do sliding board transfers from the bed to the wheelchair by myself, which a few weeks prior I declined to try. I said, "I don't need no sliding board! I'm going to get up and walk!" I'm glad I changed my thinking on that, as it was a part of the process.

I had recovery explained to me this way:
- Non-ambulatory
- Power wheelchair
- Manual wheelchair
- Walker
- Cane
- Lastly, freedom!

The reality is that not everyone that enters a rehabilitation facility has such a happy ending, as it were! Some folks stop progressing. Some folks never can walk again, but the point of rehab is to get the patient back to normal, as much as possible. Sometimes, it's a new normal, not the old normal. We, and the staff, saw a lot of miracles go back out the same doors they came in. We love and appreciate the legacy of Mr. Stan Cassidy, who had the foresight to build such a facility!

Diary entry: July 3, 2018

Todd took his last doses of lyrica and Eliquis. His nerve pain is pretty much nonexistent. and he's already been weaned off of dilaudid. It's been 3 months since Todd's blood clot in his leg. DVT. so now he can be weaned off of Eliquis.

Diary entry: July 7, 2018

Todd was amazed when he could feel his leg hairs touching the bed.

Diary entry: July 26, 2018

Todd got his whistle back

ORDER MY STEPS

Diary entry: July 17, 2018

Todd now had to do up his own pills. Part of getting more independence.

Diary entry: July 20, 2018

Todd and I went to Dairy Queen. Todd In his motorized wheelchair and I walking with him. It was our first time into a fast-food restaurant since he was struck down with GBS.

Diary entry: Aug 1, 2018

Todd stood by the van for the first time in months The first step to learning to transfer to our vehicle.

Chapter 33
A Huge Step To Freedom!

Diary entry: Aug. 13, 2018

Todd had his first successful van transfer with the sliding board

I cannot explain to you how something so simple as getting into our van could bring me such joy! I had been watching our vehicle from the windows of my hospital rooms/rehab as Penny would go out, get in the van, and drive away. Each time, my heart would sink a little, as I wondered, Will I ever ride In my van again? Many days, it felt like an impossible dream, but God knew the final outcome of our journey. I was doing my part, working hard every day to get back what I had lost.

Diary entry: Aug. 14th, 2018

Todd had his first car ride. around the block. in 160 days "

I could not drive, but as long as I could get into that passenger side, that's all that mattered back then. Penny and I took small drives around town to go get a coffee or a treat. I was beginning to have more of a clear outlook on the future, even though it was uncertain when I would be back to life as normal. At least it was normalizing, a bit more each day.

Todd McGuire

How Long?

How long will this valley last? I don't know.
We've come so far and may have so far to go.
God, if He wanted, could heal in a flash.
But all that we know is we're living our dash.
Our steps have been ordered, that's plain to see
But painful experiences make us want to flee.

Our "normal's" been halted,
He's lying in bed,
But with Jesus beside us, we don't fear or dread.
We know that we will come through,
Shining like gold, with a great testimony that's yet to be told.

So, while you are waiting in life's waiting room,
Take courage, remember, Jesus will be there soon!
He still opens prison doors and sets captives free.
He still opens blinded eyes and gives victory!
The lame man can walk, and the leper is cleansed
And Jesus has healed many, time and again!

His love is a promise to you and to me,
That no matter what we go through, His Word will bring peace.
So, today if you are facing a hard trial or test,
Call upon Jesus, He will bring sweet rest.
He walks beside you, through thick and through thin
And if you stand strong, the victory you'll win!

~Penny McGuire~
April 22, 2018

Chapter 34
Never Give Up!

I had gone into the Physio Gym, looked at the parallel bars, and said, "I am coming for you!" I would look at the wall bars that I used to help me stand, and I would tell them, "I am defeating you!" I would Look at the practice staircase, and exclaim, "I am climbing over you!" I would touch the stander and declare, "I am walking away from you!"

God, determination, and a lot of hard work got me back on my feet!

I went for evening "strolls" in my wheelchair, around the parking lot, by myself. I prayed, and I encouraged myself in Lord! Even the great King David in the Bible had to get away from everything, and everyone and encourage himself in the Lord.

> And David was greatly distressed; for the people spake of stoning him, because the soul of all the people was grieved, every man for his sons and for his daughters: but David encouraged himself in the LORD his God.
> 1 Samuel 30:6

I had made it my life's mission to be an Encourager. I wanted to let everyone know how important they are! I would roll by the Nursing station and tell them, "You are awesome!" My nurses did not get the credit that they deserved. They worked so hard to take care of me, and they even took great care of Penny. We developed friendships with them that last to this day. Often, they would come into our room, and we'd chat about things. There was lots of laughter and even tears. Several times we got to pray for our staff as we held their hands. We would sing to them. Oh, we made the best of our situation. We knew that God had allowed us to be in this situation, and so, we let our light shine.

I remember one particular evening, I had five nurses at the end of my bed, as I shared how good God is and how I would not be down, forever. This whole experience was ordained for me to minister to many wonderful staff and patients. God puts people into our pathway so that we can tell them that Jesus loves and cares for them! He knows where they are! Life is not fair, but God is always good!

One of the greatest statements ever made regarding me was, "Todd makes serving God look easy. If He can do It, so can I!" I have always kept that in the forefront of my mind. Living for God is truly the best life there is! You will never be happier than when you give Him all of you and allow Him to mold and shape your life!

A statement was made to me a few years ago after a concert in Indiana, "You have to work at staying lost." You see, God is always seeking to save that which is lost! He loves you! "For the Son of man is come to seek and to save that which was lost" (Luke 19:10).

Surrender to Him, today, and allow Him to work a work in your life. You have something to offer, and He will bring that out of you, if you allow Him to. Come to Jesus, today, and

ORDER MY STEPS

let Him wash you clean. Allow Him to make you the best version of yourself! He truly does have our best interests at heart, and living for Him will never be dull or boring. It's a great life living for the Lord!

Chapter 35
Praying Friends Are Invaluable

Diary entry: Aug. 21, 2018

Evangelist Rev. Freddy Clark stopped by to pray for Todd. today We got to go on his first outing. today We went for a nice drive"

Penny and I got into our van at the entrance to the Stan Cassidy, and all of a sudden, there was our good friends, Evangelist and Mrs. Freddy Clark, from Virginia. He was in the area, holding healing services, and wanted to come by and pray for me. He laid hands on my head, then my feet, and prayed a powerful prayer. He rebuked any nerve damage and declared health in my cells, body, and life! Thank you, Jesus, for the powerful men and woman that you have placed in our path! They only had a minute or so to stay, and that's more than what God needs to do an instant miracle in your life.

We continued on to Subway to grab a quick lunch. We had to use the drive-thru, but it didn't matter. I was mobile again, or in a vehicle at least. Now, the possibilities are endless! I found that I couldn't travel too far, yet, as sitting up for even a 1/2 hour was hard and caused pain in my tailbone.

Todd McGuire

This was something that I had to work at as our home was two hours away. I would go from sitting to laying in the seat back, but thankfully, it didn't take too long to get used to the drive, again.

I was feeling so much better, and we had ramped up my therapies to 25-30 a week! I even started to work on a moose painting in recreational therapy. When you're too busy in life, you don't always have time to explore your deeper talents and abilities, and you could be robbing yourself, and others, of what you may uncover.

I actually went through grade six twice because the teachers thought I was so smart that they wanted me to stay back and teach the new students coming in. (Or, that's what I told myself!) Ok, I digress. My grade six art teacher began to see some artistic abilities and asked me if I would like to be one of a few that had been chosen to draw on some of the walls around our Perth Middle School. I agreed, especially if it was going to get me out of regular class. We drew Charlie Brown, Snoopy, and the Peanuts gang, as well as other characters.

Now, here I was, thirty plus years later, and I was uncovering untapped talents. It was so enjoyable and freeing to be able to express my feelings onto the canvas. Take the time to find out what your hidden talents are! You will not be disappointed if you hone your skills.

Chapter 36
Living On The Edge

With the warmer weather came the opportunity to be outside. Penny and I would enjoy a leisurely stroll around the block, and oft times we were joined by one or more of the rehab patients. One day, Penny and I were out, when I first got the power chair. I hadn't quite learned it's parameters, just yet. I thought it would flip me over backwards when I went uphill. Although you must be very careful, as you transition from level ground to uneven, the chairs are quite steady, a fact that I had to learn.

I was getting ready to enter a crosswalk through a cutout in the sidewalk. The other side of the road had quite a steep incline to get back onto the sidewalk. It was obvious that it was made by someone who had never been in a wheelchair. As I made my way across to the other side, Penny was there watching and coaching me, like all wives and mothers do. Keep in mind that this chair alone weighed 400 pounds and I was a trim 330 pounds at this time. That's 730 pounds that we were moving. As I approached the sidewalk incline, Penny reached out and grabbed the back of the chair to steady it, and began to exclaim loudly, "Jesus, help us," as it tipped sideways. The wheelchair balanced on its wheelie bars and Penny still called on the Lord and tryed to push me up. If the chair was going to roll, it would roll without her help, however, I did need Jesus. That was a scary moment:

the kind that clears your sinuses and you can breathe a lot better? It actually scared me, too, but I wasn't about to admit that.

We had many adventures with the power chair over that spring and summer! Another night we were out on a stroll. It was later than usual, but the evening was so incredible. As we started back to the SCCR, I could see these June bug type beetles, but smaller. They were flying up into the trees from the lawns and flower gardens. My first thought was that I hoped one of them didn't get into Penny's hair! Then, my second thought was it would be pretty cool to see how she reacts! My second thought was about to become reality. As we reached the end of our walk, with about a half a kilometer to go, one of those beetles, rose from the ground and thought that Penny's hair would make a nice place to take a rest. Let me tell you, Usain Bolt, Ben Johnson, nor any other Olympic runner could've kept up with her! As she screamed and called upon the name of Jesus, she got a hitch in her giddy'up and took off up the road, screaming all the way! Needless to say, she made it back to the facility much sooner than I.

Chapter 37
Healthier Than I've Ever Been

Diary entry: Aug. 3, 2018

"25 therapies this week. 29 miles on the scifit. standing twice a day. successful board transfers. Success with the super pole. 1/2 car transfer. beat diabetes. walking today. Also. today Todd walked around the loop at Stan Cassidy. 140 metres. over 1/10th of a kilometre. with only 2 rests using the steady mate. Banner week."

I got a super report from Dr. Smith, today. He came over from the DECH to meet me and congratulate me on becoming Diabetes free! He said, "I could've just sent the report, but I wanted to shake your hand. It's not often that I get to shake the hand of a person that has beaten diabetes!" My health had been getting increasingly better and I credit that to God, doctors, therapists, diet, and exercise. The Bible says in 1 Timothy 4:8; "… bodily exercise profits little," but it still certainly profits!

Diary entry: Aug. 24, 2018

Todd walked with a regular walker. for the first time. around the block

Todd McGuire

Diary entry: Aug. 25, 2018

Todd and I got to travel to our home in Perth for the first time. in over 7 months. and we got to sit outside under the carport. Todd couldn't enter the house yet as he couldn't do stairs.

Diary entry: Aug. 29, 2018

Todd started using the stairs. today. at SCCR

Diary entry: Sept. 3, 2018

First church service in 6 months 44th annual labour day convention service in Perth-Andover.

Diary entry: Sept. 5, 2018

Todd bought a new knee brace for his left knee injured in the taxi incident. His knee has been clicking and having pain since the incident and this seems to take the edge off the pain.

Diary entry: Sept. 11, 2018

Todd given clearance to use walker in bedroom and bathroom. only.

Diary entry: Sept. 12, 2018

Learning to maneuver in the kitchen washing dishes. Yesterday he made toast. Todd went solo with walker wheelchair and pt followed behind

ORDER MY STEPS

Diary entry: Sept. 16, 2018

Todd's first weekend home. Got to go into our house for the first time in 8 months and also got to sleep in his bed. Todd's dad and brother in law had to put shower handles in the shower and they built a little wooden piece by the flush for Todd to use to get up from it. Very low-key weekend. Stayed home and rested.

Diary entry: Sept. 20, 2018

Date night at Diplomat. Todd used his walker to get in.

Diary entry: Sep. 25, 2018

Played ping pong with Kameron and assistant. Played with wheelchair behind him.

Diary entry: Sept. 26, 2018

Todd spent time in the occupational therapy kitchen whipping up a batch of chocolate cupcakes. Tomorrow he will top them with peanut butter icing that he also whipped up.

Diary entry: Sept. 30, 2018

Todd's first time to drive. and he drove us back to the Stan Cassidy from home. The doctor had recently cleared him to drive. but he hadn't felt ready until now.

Diary entry: Oct. 6, 2018

Todd's first time in his parent's home in almost 9 months to celebrate Canadian thanksgiving.

Todd McGuire

Diary entry: Oct. 10, 2018

Todd gets stim on his right ankle that's been giving him issues.

Diary entry: Oct. 12, 2018

Todd helped kick off the Stan Cassidy Foundation Fundraiser. He spoke to a group of donors, the son of the late Stan Cassidy and staff.

Diary entry: Oct. 18, 2018

Todd's report of the mri on his knee came back. Longest report Dr. O'Connell has ever read. Tears in meniscus, baker's cysts, and a partial tear of his ACL. Also age-related arthritis.

Diary entry: Oct. 19, 2018

Todd's first time to pump gas into our van in over 7.5 months.

Diary entry: Oct. 26, 2018

Arrived home   We left for our tour, 282 days ago, and took the really long way home

Diary entry: Nov. 2, 2018

Kismet photography gave us the gift of a photo shoot at the Castle in Perth, to celebrate our journey with GBS

ORDER MY STEPS

Diary entry: Nov. 11, 2018

First time to preach. Preached in Upper Kent. Had to sit on walker. Did a fabulous job

Diary entry: Nov. 14, 2018

Todd's first time on treadmill. Was on 3 minutes. Did very well.

Diary entry: Nov. 20, 2018

Todd received his 16th and final IVIG treatment.

Diary entry: Dec. 7, 2018

Todd had his first post release appointment with Dr. O'Connell. All muscle groups are working. Upper body is fully back. feet are still somewhat weak. Upper body and lower body reflexes are firing.

Diary entry: Dec. 5, 2018

Got to sing for the Premier In the first part of December. we started back to a limited touring of concerts.

Diary entry: Dec. 31, 2018

X-ray on right ankle that's been giving him problems since the taxi incident.

Diary entry: Jan. 6, 2019

Getting back more feeling in his feet. weekly. Sometimes he will walk around inside the house without a cane. or he'll just use one cane in the house. His energy levels are still not 100, but they are on their way.

Diary entry: Jan. 16, 2019

We retired Todd's walker, and he's walking with the aid of only one cane now.

Diary entry: Feb 20, 2019

Todd's getting more feeling back in his hands and feet. Now able to feel the bottom of his feet when he walks. He walks mostly without a cane now, in the house.

Diary entry: March 20, 2019

Todd's third emg.

Diary entry: July 10, 2019

Todd's last day of outpatient therapy

This trial had an expiry date! Day 492: That was the day that I had been looking forward to since day 1! I was like a soldier in a battle that I didn't ask to fight in; a battle arena that I entered into and truly didn't know what the final outcome would be. It could've taken my life. I didn't know how long it would last. There was no way out, just go ahead.
- 492 days I stayed on the battlefield.
- 492 days I swung my sword.
- 492 days I got up and pressed on.
- 492 days I fought fear.
- 492 days I fought pain, anxiety, and depression.
- 492 days I climbed, I pressed on. I looked to the Author and the Finisher of my faith.

ORDER MY STEPS

God spoke to me at the beginning of this trial and said that my steps were ordered. It was ultimately my steps that I lost, due to becoming paralyzed, but it wasn't until I lost my ability to walk that God moved in and carried me. He truly is a friend that sticks closer than a brother! He became my sword and my shield! He gave me the strength and stubborn tenacity to go on, one day at a time. And, in the middle of my battlefield, I found a peace that truly passed all my understanding! When I should've gone down, He brought me up! When I should've faltered, He taught me to endure and to press on!

I know that not every GBS soldier has a journey that turned out like mine. We have lost many a good man and woman on the battlefield. Many have been wounded beyond repair. Many bear the scars of their fierce battle.

It was Jacob of old in the Bible that wrestled with an angel of the Lord all night long. He battled. He fought. He struggled and ultimately won but not before the angel touched the hollow of his thigh, causing it to go out of joint. He left that battle never walking the same again. He was different. His once confident stride was reduced to small, careful, steady steps. His ability to run had been changed, but he won the battle, and for that he could truly thank the Lord! Jacob prevailed and his name was changed to Israel, as a result. Because he prevailed in this wrestling match, he had power with God and with men.

If you are caught in a battle today with Guillain-Barre Syndrome, cancer, sickness, or any other situation that would like to rob you of your joy and peace, my advice to you, is to keep moving on. Don't give up and don't give in! Place your life in the Master's hand and let Him carry you!

Todd McGuire

Thank you for taking the time to read my condensed story of a trial that has forever changed my life. I hope you received strength and hope from some of my stories.

I have said it so many times before, but will close the book with this statement:

"I have been to the bottom, and at the bottom, I found a rock, and his name is Jesus!"

Blessings,
Todd McGuire
1 Year, 4 Months, and 5 Days

www.ingramcontent.com/pod-product-compliance
Lightning Source LLC
LaVergne TN
LVHW021352080426
835508LV00020B/2247